False Start:

A Record of Experiences

By Tay Monét

Paperback ISBN 978-1-7355233-0-9
Kindle Edition 978-1-7355233-1-6

Library of Congress Control Number: 2020914862

Edited by The Writer's Source LLC.
Internal Formatting by Suzette Vaughn.
Cover design by Ojedokun Daniel O., IG:@danny_mediapro.
Photograph by David Small, IG: @focusontrellblazer.

Printed in the United States of America.

This paperback edition first published in 2020

Published by Tay Monét
www.taymonet.com

Dedication

In loving memory of Kenneth W. Roberts who consistently pushed me and had such an influential role and impact on my life. I'm forever grateful coach. The seeds you planted are still multiplying.

For those of us who have awaken sex before it was time, there's hope.

And to my future husband this book is dedicated to you too my love.

"I have fought the good fight, I have finished the race, I have kept the faith." 2 Timothy 4:7

Acknowledgments

First and foremost I thank God, Jesus, my Lord and savior, who placed it on my heart to write this book. When I fell short and felt unworthy the words were breathed into my spirit making it possible for this book to exist.

My family who's been there since day one:

Papa & Nana (my grandparents) who believe I can do anything, that nothing is out of my reach. Your faith is contagious. Also, thank you for tackling the task of writing my About the Author section without any hesitation.

Mom. Thank you for your strength, sacrifices, and instilling self-worth in us early on. Your support and unconditional love has not gone unnoticed.

Mallory, my younger sister, thank you for your undying support, encouraging words and providing comic relief when needed. You get me in a way only a sister can.

Hubie, my lil bro, you are a refreshing reminder that young people crave the word of God. Your hunger pushed me to get this book out sooner rather than later.

Nina, thank you for believing in me and supporting the book since I shared it with you years ago, when it was just an impression. You checked in on my progress, pushing and motivating me to get back on the saddle when I fell off.

Asia Q. your support brought me to tears. Sis, you are such a blessing and a constant reminder there's good in this crazy world.

Nette & Nemo you both checked in on my progress periodically and provided priceless support. You both are a reminder of you are who you hang around and I'm glad I can say you both are in my circle. I told you guys before and I'll say it again, I believe we're going to make boss moves.

eGroup ladies, it's too many of you all to list but you know who you are. You all constantly send positive vibes, articles, links to writer conferences and a kind word right when it was needed. Thank you so much! I was asked to write what my ladies group mean to me in a few sentences; I wrote the following: "I joined a women's group when I had recently fell out with some close friends which broke me in ways I didn't know were possible. I wanted to be left alone to mend the hurt but I knew I didn't need to be alone. I was at a low-point, friendships-wise when I joined this group not knowing I was in the process of gaining women I can truly call sisters to do life with."

To a former Ops team member, Joseph W., who checked in on my progress with the book many Sundays. Thank you so much for taking the time to share a kind word and motivate me.

Olivia W., my church team leader and friend; your check-ins help hold me accountable.

Writer's Group: Lee, thank you, thank you for thinking to include me in your new found writer's group. Being around all you talented writer's inspired me and rubbed off on me as well. You all's insight, expertise, understanding and feedback gave me the push I needed to tackle this thing head on. Thank you Brian, Dave, Lee, Lindsay and Megan. *Air hug*

The Writer's Source, the editing professionals, who were patient and accommodating to a newbie like me. You all made the editing process smooth and painless. I respect and appreciate your honesty while being proactive and encouraging. I initially cringed at the thought of undergoing this process but it was seamless.

And to the countless others who invested in me albeit emotionally, financially, mentally and/or spiritually; thank you all from the bottom of my heart I am forever grateful for each and every last one of you.

Much love,

Tay

Contents

False Start:
A Record of Experiences

Tay Monét

False Start (Google Dictionary, 11Feb2019):

- An invalid or disallowed start to a race, usually due to a competitor beginning before the official signal has been given.
- An unsuccessful attempt to begin something.

Caveat: False Starts fall in two categories, accidental and intentional. Accidental, starting before the official command due to nerves, impulse, or anticipation of the start command which is a risk. Intentional, not wanting to run the race before you, a cop out; or strategically even to charge it to the field so the next athlete that jumps the gun will be disqualified.

However, whatever you do, don't disqualify yourself.

This is a true confession of a track girl, everyone loves them right? Well let's find out.

"But know this, that in the last days grievous times shall come. For men shall be lovers of self, lovers of money, boastful, haughty, railers, disobedient to parents, unthankful, unholy, without natural affection, implacable, slanderers, without self-control, fierce, no lovers of good, traitors, headstrong, puffed up, lovers of pleasure rather than lovers of God; holding a form of godliness, but having denied the power thereof: from these also turn away. For of these are they that creep into houses, and take captive silly women laden with sins, led away by divers lusts, ever learning, and never able to come to the knowledge of the truth."

2 Timothy 3:1-7

Sounds familiar?

Introduction

I consider myself a work in progress as this life is a daily walk. The more I live this life out, I do believe I am only becoming more sophisticated, resilient and mature. I am not saying that I cross every t and dot every i but my heart is in the right place and I am willing and obedient. I have found a way to combat temptation by simply "listening to the Holy Spirit" and making smarter choices. Through trial and error, I have learned that I cannot do it all on my own. It is the leading and prompting of the Holy Spirit that sets me straight ensuring I stay on the right path.

With that said I felt a strong "pull" to become celibate. I fought it initially because it seemed daunting to me. I had the typical thoughts: what's the point? I'm not a virgin. I already had sex with him, and so on. In all honesty, I was afraid of failing because I did not know if I had the will power to follow through or even the desire. I could not shake this inner compelling to be obedient. I understood my body was a holy temple and I needed to start treating my body as such. I decided to honor God by saving myself for my husband, the God-ordained man HE has for me. I'm walking in obedience and stepping out of my comfort zone as I type out my personal, some of which are untold, secrets for the world to read. I do this because it is bigger than me and my feelings. I know this will help others as it would have helped me. In the meantime, while Mr. Right is getting himself together, I am continuously being shaped and molded into a better woman as well. We will meet in due time.

Overall, I am thankful for the experiences I have encountered because they have made me the person I am today, stronger and bolder. I have learned from the choices I've made (good and bad), each and every individual I've encountered and the consequences from said choices. As the saying goes: for every action, there is a reaction. The Holy Bible speaks on the principle of being a good steward which includes being faithful with what we have. This includes my body for it is a temple of the Lord. It is not mine but borrowed. If I am not a good steward of what I currently have why should God bless me with more? I must, therefore, show myself approved. This means being faithful with what's currently in my possession. The size of it, however, is of no importance. With my will to continue in obedience, God, in turn, multiplies the portion I have been given. Need proof? The *Parable of the Talents*, located in *Matthew Chapter 25*, epitomizes this.

Unfortunately, this does not mean we are exempt from temptation, quite the contrary. God will always present a way for us to exit, to flee from temptation. It is up to us to decide if we want to play with fire or "book it" out of there running the opposite direction. As my fam use to tell me "you play with fire you're bound to get burned." With that said, I know what things tempt me and what areas I struggle with. I must be wise and strategic to guard my heart and make more intelligent decisions. This entails not putting myself in certain situations. God will test us, to help

4

grow our faith which results in a TEST-imony. What He will not do, however, is tempt you (James 1:13-15). Temptation comes from Satan. Do not confuse the two. Allow me to further explain: A test is a series of struggles you experience that merit God stepping in on your behalf; it strengthens your walk with the Lord. This is different from temptation, which is flirting with sin. I need us all to clearly understand the difference. Remember, if we play with fire, chances are we will indeed get burned for the wages of sin is death. Don't risk it fam; too much is at stake.

"No purity, no power. Purity, boundless power" – Beth Moore, *Strongholds*

Prologue:
"Run Your Race to Win"

"One of the most important factors in reaching your goals in life is to have a single-minded focus. Don't let yourself become distracted by what others say or do. Run your race to win."

-unknown

Have you ever competed in any sports or do you consider yourself an athlete? How about a go-getter? Competitive? Do you enjoy working up a sweat and running for miles on in? Perhaps you're not a fan of long-distance running; me neither, well it depends. Okay, who am I fooling? I do enjoy working out but I absolutely HATE running extremely long distances, for now anyway (wishful thinking). I do enjoy a friendly competition. But this is not a book to discuss how physically in or out of shape we are but this is to be seen more along the lines of a metaphor. If you are familiar with the sport of Track and Field then you may have some understanding that it is quite a vigorous sport that many partake in around the globe on various levels (AAU/USA, grade school, collegiate, professional). It is one of the oldest and most respected sports to date. Track and Field tests your physical capabilities as well as your mental strength. For example, the 400-meter dash, in particular, is one of the most challenging, mentally exhausting and physically diminishing race to compete in. If you're not mentally prepared you'll count yourself out or think too highly of yourself which in turn will have a negative impact on your physical performance. The physical aspect is challenging for one, the 400-meter race is a Dash! Check any heat sheet/performance list and the event is listed as "400m Dash" not 400m RUN, but very similar to the 200m Dash and World-renowned, arguably Olympic favorite 100m Dash. Therefore the 400m is not a racewalk pace, jog, not even a run as its 800m counterpart but a full-throttle, all-out sprint.

My summer track coach used to tell his athletes to "leave it on the paint!" On our practice track, there was a "splash puddle" of dried white paint that was fixed right outside the entrance fence of the track. Any personal issues I may have been carrying albeit a bad day, high school drama, family drama, whatever that could/would distract me from having a successful and great practice, I would hear his voice echo in my conscience "leave it on the paint." If we did not get it together before stepping on the track, we were banished to the paint splotch to regroup. Similar to life, there will be some things you must release in order to give your best, sometimes it's just too much for you to carry, but that's okay because it wasn't meant for you to carry.

There is a connection between the 400m Dash and how life is to be lived. We should strive to maintain a positive perspective on life if we want to see more positive results. You attract what you are. Granted, bad things happen to good people but that is a part of life but life can shift just by how you choose to view it. In the words of Dr. Seuss, "When something bad happens you have three choices: You can either let it define you, let it destroy you, or you can let it strengthen you." However; there should also be a sense of urgency; time is of the essence for tomorrow is not promised so enjoy and do what you can with your present. We must have a desire to do our best, trusting that all those long hours of practice have prepared us for this moment. Listen to your coach and leave everything that is hindering you behind on the "paint" and let's finish this race of life, crossing our finish lines on E. With that said, let's pull out the footage and dive into my race; or in this case, False Start.

"Therefore, since we are surrounded by such a great cloud of witnesses, let us throw off everything that hinders and the sin that so easily entangles. And let us run with perseverance the race marked out for us, fixing our eyes on Jesus, the pioneer and perfecter of faith. For the joy set before him he endured the cross, scorning its shame, and sat down at the right hand of the throne of God. Consider him who endured such opposition from sinners, so that you will not grow weary and lose heart." Hebrews 12: 1-3 (NIV)

Chapter 1:
Back In The Day

"Watch! You are all going to go down and like it!" I stood my ground, giving Kelton the meanest mug as I responded, "Negative! Not ever! That is disgusting!" He chuckled and taunted us high school girls for being naïve. Kelton was an undergraduate from Clark Atlanta University. He was volunteering to coach a summer track team of kids ranging from 6-18 years old as a way of "giving back to the community." To my surprise, Kelton had a real knack for coaching. Although he was unable to execute the techniques with the precision he required from us, he was a great volunteer coach. He also proved to be very wise in the sex 101 category as well. I found this to be particularly surprising, as I did not find him very attractive. I glanced down and rubbed my abstinence bracelet, "Yeah, I'll never..." I thought to myself. Not having the guts nor the energy to continue to argue with Kelton, a "grown" ready to debate on command college student, so I decided to opt-out of this discussion.

"Kendall... Kendall! Are you listening to us?" Courtney asks slightly irritated.

I snap back into present time as I respond to Courtney in a matter of fact tone "No. No I'm not listening to you and Liyah's nonsense." We are eating dinner at Avery's, the Student-Athletes Dining Hall, and having causal dinner convo when we somehow manage to land on the topic of fellatio. The three of us are freshmen on the Track team at Taylor University better known as TU. Little did we know our track and field affiliation would form a bond like no other. I follow up with, "I've been with Lance going on four years and our sex life is just fine, there's no need to. But thank you both for your concerns." We all giggle and silly me assumes the conversation has run its course and is now over. Liyah, much to my disdain, began to demonstrate a how-to-tutorial, right on the spot.

"Girl, once you try it, you'll love it," she informs me.

"I highly doubt that" attempting to drive my point across that I was completely uninterested. Almost on cue, Lance walks in the double doors with his teammates sporting letterman jackets and baseball caps.

But before we discuss Lance let's rewind back to my upbringing.

I was a fairly good child growing up; consistently making honor roll and always wanting to do good and make my folks proud. They instilled the fear of God in me at a young age; growing up in church quoting scriptures and memorizing the books of the Bible was rewarded with fast food gift cards, cash prizes and warranted praises. With my ability to do things with such a high level of ease in tandem with my competitive nature, I found myself in the winning pool quite often. As a young child, I was known as "the entertainer," awarding me a fair amount of friends. I was funny to them. However, I was quiet in the classroom, shy rather, but once that recess bell rang I broke out of my shell. After accruing a following, becoming popular and feeling included I was informed the county was redistricting. I would be enrolling in a different elementary school come to the start of fourth grade. I was devastated and spent the majority of that summer upset. The realization that I was leaving my friends and facing the unknown made me insecure of what was to come.

Come 4th grade I hardly interacted with any of my peers as much. I distanced myself from everyone around me at my school. At the time, my mom was a young single parent with two kids, so we lived with her parents on and off again throughout my childhood which was "normal" to me growing up. I enjoyed the extra love, guidance, and everything else that came with living with my nana and papa (pronounced Paw-Paw). But there were times when my mom would move us out; therefore, my sister and I would either transfer to a new school or my mom would drive us to and from a neighboring city to the school district of my grandparents. My mom did the best she could and ensured we would receive the best education that was available to us, even if it meant waking us up at the crack of dawn and getting us ready to make the drive to school every day.

Due to the constant moving throughout grade school, I was not able to form those typical childhood friendships. That all changed when I befriended a young boy named Josh, he became my best friend by middle school. Since he lived next door to my grandparents, he was the one friend that would never leave, regardless of the school changes and moves.

By the time middle school rolled around, I was also starting to hang around a group of girls that would be considered "fast" and I'm not talking about track speed. I wasn't 'bout that life. This was, in part, due to the efforts of my youth group at church whose leaders were adamant about abstinence. I still remember one leader saying, "Don't let a few minutes of your life ruin your life." They really knew how to scare us. For those not familiar with the term, abstinence, as any Google search will inform you, is a self-enforced restraint from indulging in bodily activities; in this particular case, sexual activities. The whole point was to teach us to value our bodies and save ourselves for our future spouse; as God had intended for us to enjoy sex in holy matrimony. These two girls I spent the most time with were bizarrely hell-bent on us losing our virginities together. They went as far as to devise a plan that we would all stay the night at Jessica's house where it would happen . Jessica and Ashley had boyfriends who they were infatuated with but I on the other hand wanted no part of the secret mission. I wasn't even thinking about a boyfriend, yet along fantasizing about sex. I came up with some bogus excuse as to why I wouldn't be able to show up that weekend, stating I was still hurting from a dirt bike incident that took place days earlier at Jessica's house. After a weekend and a handful of 3-way calls passed by, we all met up with one another at school. They talked about their weekend festivities while I listened, providing zero input or feedback. I was slightly confused about whether they had lost their virginities or not.

Jessica changed the topic and said, "Aye we should all tryout for the track team." We were in the 8th grade yet I had never even heard about the team or sport until that moment. I figured, I'm fast, sure why not, what do I have to lose?" The three of us tried out, which turned out to be more rigorous than any of us anticipated. The tryouts were conducted over three days which entailed the timing of various running events and trying out different field events.

The squad list was posted in the common area by the conclusion of the school week. We walked towards the girls' sheet as some girls walked away all smiles and others in tears. I became nervous as I didn't realize how serious this roster list was. Ashley finds her name first then I locate mine. Jessica didn't make the cut. She was so upset. It became difficult to be happy for Ashley and

I. "Wow, she's the one who suggested we all tryout and she didn't even make it. It was her idea!" I thought to myself. Track was not even on my radar but is testament to the saying, "what is meant to be will be."

As the season went on, I began to really enjoy track. Running on relays and being apart of a team made me feel like I belonged. I had never been a part of an organized team and I had only played with the boys on my block playing street races, football, tag and riding bikes. It was safe to say I was a tomboy and was proud of it. I was running off pure talent. By the time track came around the following year, I was in high school with new friends thanks to county redistricting again and was gaining attention from local coaches, with requests to join their summer track clubs.

My high school friends were boy crazy and they solely talked about whom they were dating and/or sleeping with. I was focused on school and track so I was deemed the "good girl" but was still cool enough to hang with. I got along with everyone (for the most part), I had a sense of humor and was a student-athlete that was talented and down to earth. Apparently more people knew me and were interested in me than I had realized. I always found it odd how well known I was as I didn't partake in any parties, sleepovers, or hangouts my freshman year as track started to consume my time. Having two practices a day and then taking on a part-time job occupied the majority of my time. But my focus started to shift when I met Lance the summer after my freshman year.

Chapter 2:
Where I Wanna Be

Lance was a talented baseball player, with professional offers in his future. Not only did he think he was superman, he walked around this 40,000+ population size campus with the confidence to match. I met Lance back in high school, although we attended two different schools, we were high school sweet hearts. He ran summer track and played baseball for Carver Academy. Lance was a very handsome young man and an all-around amazing athlete. You name it, he could do it. By the end of track season, my 9th grade track season, I was being approached by different summer AAU/USA league coaches to run for them. I was fairly new to this whole "track world"; however, I decided to run with one of my HS teammates' summer team. I trusted her judgment. She was an A-honor roll student who won homecoming queen and held many accolades hence why I felt her guidance was sound advice. But it's key to note: Through all of

14

this, I have learned that people may have the best intentions but their "best intentions" can lead you straight to hell. Remember that.

My first day of summer track practice was intense but being the competitor that I am, I'm always up for a challenge. At that time in life, I was still pretty shy so I shadowed the few folks I knew which were basically my high school teammates. Halfway through the first week of practice, I was approached by a handsome young man. This guy asked to borrow my phone in order to call his mom for a ride home from practice. After making the call, he hands the phone back and tells me his name is Lance. He then explains how he accidentally left his phone at home. He appeared to be genuine and he fit the bill of someone of a careless yet harmless nature. I learned early on that Lance was the clown of the team, he joked with any and everyone! No one was off limits. But when he asked to use my phone he seemed open and genuine...vulnerable in a sense. I didn't think anything of it and went my way after he made his phone call. Later that night I received a phone call from Lance, go figure. It was all staged to get my number. I felt naïve but was slightly impressed. I was 14 at the time and never would have devised such a plan to get some one's digits. He had skills in my young eyes with that stunt.

We continued our conversation from earlier that day and as with the calls becoming more frequent so they started to grow in the length of time. We were officially in the all too familiar "puppy dog" stage of love. Neither one wanting to hang up, sending good morning text messages to each other, and falling asleep on the phone together. No one could convince us that we would ever break up; we just knew that this was a forever thing. As the summer track season came to an end, our love for one another had blossomed. We were always supportive of one another despite attending two different high schools located in two different cities. I would attend his Friday Night football games and baseball games accompanied by his family. He ended up giving up track to focus on baseball but he still would come to support me at my meets.

I fell for Lance hard. He was my supporter on and off the track. I confided in Lance, sharing my deepest thoughts, goals, and desires with him. I trusted him completely, with no limit; I was sure I was in love with him, I'm talking Mary J's real love.

One evening, while traveling back from a successful Indoor Nationals making our way down the winding roads of Tennessee in the back of Coach Smith's sedan, Julian and I discussed "the moment" often referred to as "my v-card." Julian, better known as Juelz, was a very close friend of mine. Juelz and I trained together, competed together, traveled together, and partied together. We ran our high school career together forming a sibling-like bond. Julian was the type of person to give you the coat off his back if he was fond of you. He kept everyone laughing at all times, even during inappropriate moments. Julian, was also quite opinionated. You were sure to know his thoughts and receive a piece of his mind whether or not you asked for it. A few hours into the drive back home, after relishing the excitement and glee of both of us earning All-American honors, the achievement high had eventually worn off. Coach Smith was conversing with his friend who tagged along on the road trip. The music is up high enough to muffle the various convos that are commencing. Juelz and I are sitting in the last row of the SUV discussing whether or not we'll have an off day from practice.

Julian abruptly asks "Have you and Lance done it yet?"

I was thrown off by the drastic subject change but not too dumbfounded due to the person posing the question. "Yet?!" I thought to myself. But I answered Juelz, "No, we haven't but he has brought it up. He hasn't pressured me."

Juelz turned to me in shock and looked me intensely in my eyes and said "Girl, what are you waiting on?! How long have you guys been together? Over a year, correct? You've made him wait long enough, girl give him some tonight!" I laugh at Juelz and waived it off; but little did he know that I had been pondering the idea myself. I was on the fence but Juelz may have just swayed me. I was teetering back and forth; mulling it over and over again. My upbringing and beliefs had me torn, let me explain...

As I mentioned prior; my church-attending, God serving, fervently praying family had instilled in me the values I held so dearly and upheld as law. I had been taught to wait until marriage. It was imparted in me to practice abstinence. However, the peer pressure around me was booming! The vast majority of my closest friends, at the time, had already lost their virginity. As time progressed I became less aware of my stance on abstinence. It became less of a priority as the sexual fantasies started rolling in. One of my homegirls would discuss her rendezvous with upperclassmen while we worked on group activities in Spanish class. With so many people seemingly doing it, the "wrongness" of it started to diminish; it became the norm while abstinence became the abnorm. I started to justify, in my mind, why not waiting wasn't such a big deal with thoughts like: "We're getting married anyway. He loves me. It's okay, you love him and he loves you." But hindsight is real. They say experience is a great teacher but wisdom – learning from other's experiences – will save you time.

I was a junior in high school and was still a virgin. I wasn't ashamed of my virginity but I wasn't particularly proud. Not realizing that everyone was wanting to fit in in high school, I truly wasn't the odd man out but I sure felt like it. I wasn't one to appear at the house parties or have sleepovers but I was well known due to my athletic abilities being broadcast on the morning speaker announcements, newspaper articles and local evening news appearance. I didn't really hang-out outside of school as I was dedicated to track, keeping good grades and well, Lance. I started to feel as if I was missing out on something that my virginity was keeping me from, if I were to have my friends tell it anyway. I mustered up the courage to shoot Lance a text message telling him I was ready. He called me back asking me if I was sure. I told him with confidence that I was ready and how "he better lay it down." I clearly did not know what I was asking for as I was an ill-informed virgin and Lance was not. This wasn't his first rodeo. That lowkey bothered me but my friends assured me that having someone experienced is "better."

He kept up his end of the bargain. While in the moment, I laid in his bed in pain, sweating and paranoid as I had snuck out of my house. The pain became too much prompting me to call a time out, I needed a water break to regroup. I was eating the words of my trash talk I spewed just hours before. I was expecting a special moment of tender intimacy but I received pain and a few "You want me to stop?'s". But the fighter in me thugged it out. With a couple of timeouts and a Caprisun scattered throughout I made it through. Again...hindsight.

Four to five months pass by and Lance and I were sitting in his car of my driveway. He wanted to call it quits because he was going away for college. I had never felt so used and abandoned. I didn't want to cry in front of him as I felt he didn't deserve to see my tears but the harder I tried to hold them back, they only flowed more relentlessly. Here I was, sitting in the passenger seat of his car, in my driveway, from yet another Bedroom Boom Session. Convenient timing, right? At this point, I was in too deep and I had invested too much of myself. I had put a strain on my mother and I's relationship while I was sneaking out of the house to see Lance. In retrospect, this probably was some horrible déjà vu for her. I had become his puppet. Whatever he wanted I was there to provide albeit mentally, physically and emotionally. I was blindsided by the breakup. I want to say I left that blue mustang with what little dignity I had but unfortunately, I needed clarity. I couldn't find the words to adequately portray my hurt, so the tears kept flowing.

Hindsight: I had jumped the gun. I thought I could have the best of both worlds. I did what I wanted when I wanted not calculating the long term effects. I thought I found a loophole that enabled me to do as I please and still receive the promises God had for me, but I reaped what I sowed. Despite the strings I tried to pull or excuses I created, deep down I knew I was in the wrong. The self-inflicted feeling of unworthiness undoubtedly caused me to distance myself from church as I didn't feel clean enough. Forgetting you're invited to come as you are. My self-centeredness led me to heartache, feeling betrayed, used, unloved and less than. My poor management of temptation led me to hitting rock bottom, feeling worthless.

Once I dabbled in it once the more frequent it seemed to become and the less guilt I started to feel. I begin to sense I lost my value so I declined to hold out the next time and it just became an endless cycle. I gave myself to this notion, believing this was my only available reality. Anyone else who has been sucked into this lie: You're valuable, you are loved and you have been redeemed. I'm speaking from experience. The race does not end here.

Chapter 3:
Scared of Lonely

Upon arrival to college, I gained a roomie of whom I ended up seeing a total of three to four times that academic year. This was because I stayed up under Lance 24/7. Yes, unfortunately, I was that girlfriend. And yes, we were still together despite the driveway event I mentioned in the previous chapter. After we had a conservation consisting of me guilt tripping him about my virginity, or lack thereof, he informed me one of his male family members recommended a clean breakup but how he regretted it. Within a week we were back together and it was as if the incident never occurred. My freshman year, for the most part, revolved around Lance. I missed out on house parties, teammate gatherings and overall freshman year experience. I would go to class, practice then straight to Lance's apartment. It was like clockwork. I thought I was living the life being able to have access to him whenever I wanted. Let us emphasize the word, "thought."

I was smothering him with my antics because I was young and blindly in "*love*." I was under the impression he enjoyed my unfaltering presence as he never told me otherwise. He strongly advised me not to attend the house parties thrown by the football players stating "girls get raped there." I was convinced, borderline brainwashed, that I would end up being a date rape victim by the end of the night; so I never attended any of the football parties with Liyah and Courtney.

Around this time, the upperclassmen had amassed a name for the women's track team. According to this Gossip site titled *The Tea on Campus* (TTOC), which was utilized by various college students, so conveniently organized by the name of various Universities/Schools, would spill all the tea. Per TTOC, the track team had some hoe tendencies; Oh, what luck. I'm a freshman but a part of a team with such a reputation. But wait, there's more, Liyah and Courtney managed to make the list as well (as true freshmen I might add) but for the following: Liyah wore Baby Phat and Apple Bottom jeans too much, apparently and Courtney was considered to be a football groupie but jokes on them, she was around the football team more than the average female because her uncle was the Offensive Coordinator. I took this PSA as a personal attack and made sure it was understood that I was taken and faithful. I knew it would be an uphill battle being associated with the track team and the stigma that comes along with it. Even though the track team was loved by many that cloud that hovered made each of us guilty by association despite the fact most were monogamous and stayed in their own lane. Because of the reputation there was discord between the newcomers and the oldheads of the Women's Track Team. The rookies didn't have any tolerance for nonsense and the oldheads were stuck in their ways so there was plenty of bumping of heads. Although there was internal beef, we had each other's back if any outsider tried it with any of us. We were a family, a dysfunctional one, but a family nonetheless.

By the time my sophomore year rolled around, three of my teammates and I decided to get an apartment together off campus. It was conveniently close to Lance's apartment so that was an added bonus for me. I started to stay at my place more which prompted him to come to me instead. But the visits casually began to taper off, becoming less and less frequent. I questioned Lance on his disappearance act but he always had an answer along the lines of:

"I decided to hang with the fellas…"

"I fell asleep. Practice did me in."

"I wasn't around my phone…"

Once again, I was young and naïve, so I bought into his lies; I wanted to believe him, so I did but there was always that "iffy" feeling and thought in the back of my mind that he was hiding something.

Chapter 4:
Girl with the Tattoo

Today was just a typical day, or so I thought. The day started off with morning lifts, class, a little rehab and practice. After practice I made my way to the training room, as I normally do, to complete my 15 minutes of cold tub immersion. This day was different because I was in a rush, so I opted for an ice wrap instead. As I was getting wrapped around my quads and hamstrings, this gorgeous young man walks into the training room. He had beautiful short curly hair and was wearing jeans and a black cotton polo jacket. We instantly made eye contact but I immediately looked away once I reminded myself what my "after-practice" disheveled appearance looked like. I had just been running in the blazing sun and our coach had the "ingenious" idea of doing stadium drills before and after our intense sprint workout. As soon as I finished getting ice wrapped by our trainer I made my way back to one of the training tables to gather my belongings that were in a disarray. While stowing my items in a drawstring bag I can see from my peripheral that I was being approached by one of the men's basketball team trainers.

"Okay, this is awkward," I thought to myself as we had never really paid any attention to one another.

I finish gathering my things when he tapped me on the shoulder. I turn around and timidly yet jokingly he tells me as he clears his throat, "umm...sorry to bother you, but that guy that just walked through thinks you're gorgeous." I look over to the athletic trainers' office and see the university's star basketball player looking in my direction in full laughter instead of the fine young man that was once there. I kindly thanked the trainer for delivering the message, with a light laugh, and headed to the Women's Track and Field locker room. I quickly showered, snatched my book bag in order to make it to my Biochem lab on time. I frantically put my practice clothes from the day on a clothes loop and make my way to the dirty bins, cutting through the training room again. I round the corner passing the cold tubs. I make another left into the dim lit hall of the coaching staff and, to my surprise, there stands Mr. Gorgeous halfway down the hall. As we make our way down the hall, closer to one another, he stammers to say something, but the only words he managed to muster up were "I think you're so pretty, can we exchange numbers?" I laugh and inform him that he didn't even ask my name. He sheepishly apologized, "You're right. My name is Bryant and yours?"

"My name is Kendall. Nice to meet you, Bryant." I respond as I reach out to shake his hand. He goes to shake my hand then attempts to engage in more conversation but I cut him short in order to make it to my lab on time. I apologize as I take down his number, rushing off to get to the other side of campus leaving Mr. Gorgeous in the poorly lit hall in suspense.

From that moment, Bryant and I kept in contact. When we would text on occasion, he would inform me that he wanted to hang out. I would always remind him I was in a relationship but I was open to the idea of being friends. Bryant did not push the issue but would remind me of his presence, from time to time by way of a simple text. He kept in touch. One warm late afternoon, after spending the bulk of the day at Lance's baseball tourney, Lance decided to take out his frustrations on me as the baseball team had lost a close game. He was so cold and rude to me despite my various attempts to cheer him up. He complained about how the officials were making terrible calls and how the team should have come out with a victory. I agreed with him and I even reminded him that his team still had a chance to make it to regionals, attempting to be encouraging and remind him to look on the bright side. He wanted no part of my input. He told me he wanted to be left alone so I granted him his request.

Feeling rejected and unappreciated, I turned to someone who would appreciate me, Bryant. I was bored and had no one to talk to. Liyah was with her boyfriend and my other teammates took a road trip to another college. I opted to stay back and support Lance. It was just me, alone.

After mulling it over, debating whether or not to invite Bryant over; I sent him a text asking if he was busy. He replied remarkably quick, so I eventually extended him an invite over to my place. He arrived in record time, with a call asking where to park because our guest spots were currently occupied. Go figure, it was booty call hours. Once parking was situated, I gave him my apartment number and ended the call. I was wearing a red cami and white shorts with red trimming that read "Laguna Beach" on the upper right thigh. When I heard a knock, I hurriedly went to open the door after dimming the lights and putting on a specific playlist I had on standby to set the mood. When I opened the front door, I'm greeted with a hug and a smile. In the middle of the embrace, he tells me "You smell good." I grab his hand and lead him to the kitchen, past Liyah's room, through the living room and we further proceeded into my room. He sits on my bed and starts small talk while I sit on my desk chair facing him, just taking the entirety of this moment in, every word, every second, every racing thought.

My thoughts were cut off by his words.

"I didn't think you were going to ever invite me over."

I giggle at the truth in his statement but I reply "You seem like a pretty cool dude."

He cracks a sly smile and then continues to talk. I cut the lights off and sit on the bed next to him. The screen of my laptop was the only light projecting in my room but it was just enough. He leans in with a kiss and I'm hit with the hard fact that this is the first person I have kissed since Lance, since high school. I'm shocking my own self that I'm allowing this to happen but I don't stop Bryant, allowing the moment to continue. He picks me up and lays me higher on the bed. Then he begins to slide my shorts down, now I am becoming nervous as Lance is the only person I've been with, ever. After tossing my shorts to the floor, he starts to kiss my inner thighs and around my navel, teasing me. I hear the words *"The Girl with the Tattoo"* while my hip tattoo catches the small glimpse of light that makes it over his torso. He kisses my tat and goes back down. At this point, the guilt and shame has vanished. I have entered a state of arousal and pure bliss, for the moment. Once we finished, I told him I enjoyed his company and that I would talk to him later because I was tired. He gathered his belongings and headed for the door. After walking to the entrance he turns around and asked me to hit him up. I smiled and told him I would catch up with him as I closed the door behind him.

The next day, I went on with my normal routine as if nothing happened. From then on, the text messages from Bryant started to become more frequent. He was suddenly wanting something deeper from me, which I could not emotionally provide. I kept reminding him I was in a relationship, in which, he would respond by reminding me that I wasn't happy or I wouldn't have done what I did. Touché. He was right in a sense, I wasn't completely happy with Lance but I wasn't ready to throw away my high school love, our race was not quite over. I felt bad for the betrayal I committed and wondered how or if I would ever tell Lance about that moment. I kept living this lie attending school, practices, track meets, and dating Lance as if nothing happened. I started to ignore Bryant's messages figuring if I don't answer things would calm down. I told myself I would not do that again. I proceeded to carry on and tell no one, not even my best friend Liyah.

Chapter 5:
My Little Secret

I cannot believe what I just read! I stare at Lance's phone in disbelief. A text from one of my male teammates reads: "Aye, you trying to see about these girls?" I knew it all along but to see physical proof made it real. It broke my heart. I was infuriated. I wanted revenge. I went back into Michelle's apartment and sunk into her couch; just sitting in complete darkness, sulking in my lonesome and betrayal. This man was cheating.

Before this realization; Michelle and I were having our typical girl's night, homemade margaritas and girl talk. We were teammates and our boyfriends were teammates so we saw each other a lot but we enjoyed the bonding time. This night was interrupted with a call from her boyfriend, requesting she come pick him up from his teammate's house. I rode with her thinking

Lance would accompany him as he had yet to respond to a single text or call since this afternoon. I was a little worried.

When we pulled up we realized it was a full-blown out of control house party. Imagine my surprise as Lance informed me earlier that "it's just a team gathering." Jay hops in the car and hands me Lance's phone, I'm sure he had instant regret once the phone was in my hands, but he informed me that Lance had passed out drunk. Jay, for the record, is honest and a stand-up guy. We ride back to Michelle's apartment without Lance, leaving him to sleep off his drunkenness in the care of his remaining teammates. Lance's phone sits in my hand, fuming at the lie Lance told me, it just kept replaying in my head: "It's just the team, playing cards and whatnot." I decide to wait until I had some privacy before going into his phone. I stood in the breezeway, asking Michelle to leave the front door unlocked once Jay went inside. I unlock Lance's phone and the gut feeling I was questioning for so long was finally confirmed in a single message. I was in the acceptance stage of grief, because I was in denial for a while. Also, my betrayal came to mind but nevertheless it did not lessen the blow. All my other friends are out partying or either boo'd up. I decided it would be best if I did not bombard their passive, fun-filled evenings with my drama. I re-enter Michelle's place, plop on the couch and look at my phone. Various missed messages. One message, in particular, was from Tyson. I thought, "How timely." I decided to entertain him.

I met Tyson, get this, via social media. Crazy at the time, as it was not the norm it is now or at least it wasn't talked about. Don't judge. Anywho, I was just minding my business, tweeting per usual, when I received a DM, direct message, from him. The message was random and caught me off guard. His approach was intriguing. His conversation kept me wanting more. We ended up exchanging numbers and became "texting buddies." We spoke on the phone from time to time but he knew I was in a relationship and he "respected" that. We were homies. He told me how he noticed me in Avery's student-athlete study/dining hall but was always too shy to say anything and figured it was futile due to the fact that I had a boyfriend, so he never took his shot.

Tyson would playfully inform me of the things he would do to me if I was to ever let him. I have to admit, it turned me on, especially while being emotionally neglected by Lance; however, I would always shut Tyson down flirtatiously. Looking back, I was playing with fire. Tyson was a DE weighing 265 pounds and 6'3. Although he was massive on paper he was a huge teddy bear in person. He came equipped with a northern accent and a New Yorker attitude to match. He had a crew but for the most part he kept to himself. We kept communicating via text and the conversations grew to become longer and deeper. It got to the point I no longer saw an issue shooting him a text at 3 in the morning. I became comfortable in the mess I had created.

Fast forward to present time…

I send Tyson a text asking if he is still up. He responds before I have time to grasp exactly what is truly playing out, what I was initiating. I ask him if I could come by over-explaining to him that I was nearby at Michelle's and had been drinking but was now bored. The next message I received was Tyson's room number, "222." I gather my pride and broken heart and headed towards Michelle's front door. Stealthy and quietly I close the door behind me, ensuring I leave the door unlocked for my anticipated return. Conveniently for me, Tyson resided in the same apartment complex, "The U" rightfully named, as Michelle's apartment was only on the other side of the complex. The units were connected forming a U-shaped building enclosing a pool and clubhouse. The parking deck adjoining the back end of the seven-story U separated a nearby student-living complex. I make my way to Tyson's with revenge on my mind. This time, I was not experiencing guilt but retaliation, payback was about to commence.

I text Tyson, "I'm at the door" in hopes to prevent being seen by his roommate or alert a neighbor by a knock at the door. He replies "come in, it's unlocked. Room on your left." I take a deep breath at the front door and enter, leaving all my morals and feelings at his doorstep.

As I enter Tyson's room I see nothing but a bed, he had the biggest bed in the apartment complex that I had seen. As I walk towards his bed -noticing COD on pause- he asks, "What do I owe this visit?" I shrug and casually tell him "I figured I'd stop by, I was in the area." He chuckles as I sit down beside him on his bed. "Yeah, okay. You've never been over here before and considering the time..." He sharply interrupts himself "You know I've always wanted to have you." He looks at me with a cunning smile. I smile back and gracefully fall back on his bed allowing his comforter to connect with my backside and hips which are slightly exposed as my t-shirt rose to my waist. My top raised just enough to display my lower abdomen. He kisses my hips with gentleness.

I undo my jeans as I kick off my black and silver air max 90's, watching them roll across the floor a short ways. Tyson wasted no time. His go for the kill demeanor was a turn on. He was in a zone; I could feel his passion, his anticipation. I inched up higher on the bed and he went right along with me. I take off my shirt, with my bra remaining intact. He simultaneously tosses his white beater to the ground. He is now bare-chested adorning only some football training shorts. Thoughts raced through my mind:

Should I do this?

What am I getting myself into?

Am I acting on impulse? Feelings?

I interrupt my indecisiveness and convince myself this could be our secret, no one would have to know. Convincing myself that if I had been confiding in him all this time, why would he betray me now? I had forgotten that what's done in the dark always come to the light.

As we're both caught up in the heat of the moment, with sweat pouring and shallow breaths he states "Next time, don't make me wait so long." I'm unable to utter a response as my mouth moves but no sound comes out. We both lay in his bed with our minds blown, just lying in silence.

After I find the strength to stand and get dressed, I slip back into Michelle's place with the heavy burden of shame. It's close to sunrise, the birds are chirping and I'm just laying my head to rest about to reencounter the night's event in REM sleep.

Chapter 6:
House Party

A few months have passed. I text Tyson from time to time but I've been trying to avoid seeing him in person. So far so good. In my head, if I don't see him I don't have to face what I did. Yet again, I didn't tell my best friend, Liyah. Liyah was on the straight and narrow, giving me good girl vibes while reminding me of my younger self. She was regularly attending church, inviting me every so often but I was not trying to confront my demons just yet. I was having too much fun. Michelle had her suspensions but couldn't prove it. There are car honks outside my window. I shoot Charity a text, "I'm on my way." I grab my keys and mixed drink and head out the front door. I climb into Charity's jeep while the ultimate "doing it for the 99 and the 2000s" playlist is blasting from the stereo. Bianca, Nicole, Olivia, Courtney, and Sasha were all lit. We were anticipating this house party. Some Clark Atlanta track boys were hosting the party as one of the athlete's parents had a rental home that was a convenient distance from our campus, in a nice little suburb outside of Athens, approximately 25 minutes from TU. We drove down the longest, windiest roads ever; finally arriving to this huge house in the middle of nowhere. Cars bilaterally lined the street but we managed to find a park close by. I call Kevin to let us in as the party was invite-only. He comes to the door and greets us all with hugs. We follow Kevin downstairs to the basement where he handed us a surplus of shots to accommodate the mixed drinks we toted with us. Mike, one of Kevin's teammates, brings out a deck of cards and lay them in the center of a table off to the side. Kevin and Mike start placing bottles of alcohol on the table, brown and white alike; to entice us to come to the table. Mike is high as a kite so Kevin steps in and explains the drinking game, *High or Low*, they have set up for my teammates & I to play. Needless to say, after a few rounds of playing our little game, I am feeling good and ready to twerk this thang. The DJ, another one of Kevin's teammates, is on point with the music selections. He plays a mix of everything encompassing twerking, slow grinding and reggae.

Later on that night I went out on the patio to grab some fresh air and escape the party for a second. Shortly after, I noticed the presence of another human approaching me, it was the DJ. We chatted for a little while and I could tell he was lowkey feeling me. He was an attractive guy which kept the convo going, for me at least, until I was pulled back into the party by Charity.

Somehow in a matter of what felt like seconds, I am dancing on Kevin. Kevin and I were born and raised from the same area, different cities but repped the same area code. We had some history prior to college, mostly innocent flirting, nothing deep. We came to know one another through track although we never ran on the same team. We were talented enough to catch each other's attention at various meets over the years. Right now I am going to work on Kevin while my teammates hype up the moment I leave Kevin on the ground noticeably aroused.

After a brief moment, as I am talking to Charity he approaches me from behind to ask if he can steal me away for a few minutes. I excuse myself from Charity and two other chicks whom we were conversing with, one being a former student-athlete and her civilian friend. Pause. Let me break down the term civilian. We, TU student-athletes, refer to "regular" students as civilians. I'm not entirely sure how the term came about but it stuck through my entire college career. This particular civilian has a secret that is bound to become exposed in due time but that's a story for another time.

Kevin leads me into a bathroom where he sits me on the marble countertop. He starts kissing on me. The spontaneity of it all excites me. He pulls out a condom and in the process of putting it on when we hear loud knocks on the door. My teammates are banging on the door and are demanding the door to be opened, we look at each other; I shrug and say "ignore it." He proceeds to get undressed and I drunkenly watch him in a daze. We feel a swift breeze as the door bursts open. My teammates somehow manage to get into a locked bathroom, as for one, they know I'm in a relationship. Two, they don't know Kevin and I have history. Thirdly, for all they know I'm faithful, but drunk, but again, I had not shared my sexcapades with anyone outside of my accomplices so my friends only acted accordingly. They quickly, with no hesitation, remove me from the sink and zip up my half-unbuttoned shorts; just leaving Kevin baffled, shirtless and titillated.

As the night wines down, I hop back into Charity's jeep to go home, but it was not the same group that I rode with as the original carpool had dispersed, some left with their boyfriends. We had new additions (other teammates and a Clark Atlanta dude). While getting situated we see car lights quickly approaching the jeep's left side. People are yelling for the driver to stop. Charity's car is not even cranked to pull off. We all are shook, there's absolutely no time to react and it appears everyone is about to catch an L, perhaps their last. The oncoming car screeches and slides to a halt just in time causing the two vehicles to avoid a collision. The DJ hops out frantically to apologize to the bewildered women who were screaming, cursing and just plan scared.

"I'm so sorry, my dad told me to get that fix" he pleads. "My guy, you almost took out half of TU's track team" a bystander blurts. Everyone busts out laughing except the DJ, he is still apologizing but everyone is fine. We all start to pull out and head back to our respective places.

I'm dropped off at my place and start to make my way up the steps to my apartment. I heard footsteps behind me while noticing Charity's jeep is leaving. I turn around and not surprised that it is Kevin tailing behind me up the steps. "Is it cool if I stay with you tonight?" he asks. I respond, "I guess so, I mean your boys have already pulled off behind Charity." I unlock my door and he enters in behind me.

Chapter 7:
One Missed Call

The next morning Kevin and I awake to heavy knocks that resemble police about to knockdown the front door. I run to the peephole and witness an angry Lance on the other side. I go into instant panic mode and dash back to my bedroom to grab my phone. The lock screen is filled with multiple unanswered calls and disregarded text messages. I whisper to Kevin that my boyfriend is outside, instructing him to get dressed and call his boys to come get him. Lance is hollering at the front door and calling my phone simultaneously. I ignore both. I help gather Kevin's belongings and push him into Liyah's vacant room, telling him to lock the door. Without question, Kevin grabs his things and head into Liyah's room. I start to pace back and forth in the living room trying to devise a plan to rectify the situation at hand. While in the midst of brainstorming the best case scenarios, I hear a rummaging on my balcony. I make my way to the back and peak through an ever-so-slightly raised shade of the blinds hanging over my balcony door. To my amazement, Lance's best friend, CJ had climbed up to my patio and was hopping the railing onto the platform. I ensure the balcony's door is locked and slide into my room attempting to figure a way out of this. After a few minutes of mulling it all over, I came to the conclusion that I would just wait it out.

Approximately thirty minutes later, but what felt like forever, in complete silence, I told Kevin to have his homeboy meet him up the street from my apartment complex. Trying to convince Kevin to jump the balcony, he refuses as he has NCAA's coming up and did not want to risk being injured. The way Lance's rage is set up he might not see another day regardless, yet alone nationals. Understanding his reservations, I advise Kevin to go down the front steps but to turn and take the back entrance once at the bottom of the steps entering the breezeway. He nods his head signaling he understands and heads out the front door. I wait to hear a commotion but I hear nothing. About an hour later I hear another knock on the door. I quickly answer thinking I am in the clear. I plan on telling him that I had a mean hangover and my phone was on silent. Before I can even form the words for my pre-prepared lie Lance asks me "Why was Kevin here?"

Wait. I'm back in panic mode. I wasn't ready for that curveball. He saw him? What?!

It turns out Lance had caught Kevin heading out the back way but Lance was unable to hawk him down.

He demands again, "Why was he in your f****** apartment?!"

He rattles off another question before I can assemble an answer, "Did he spend the night?!" Lance's interrogation is intense. Instead of coming clean, the lies flowed from my mouth, word vomit: "he stayed the night but he slept on the couch. He needed a place to crash for the night." I lie, I was purely afraid I was going to lose Lance, my high school sweetheart, my first, my love. The lie I spewed out came straight from the dome, out of impulse. Even though I am fed up with him, I did not want us to end like this. He looks at me with such intensity. I maintain eye contact in an attempt to salvage any hope of him believing me. He starts to relax; I as well taking a seat in my desk chair. I'm nervous contemplating what words may leave my mouth next that I don't even realize that I'm fidgeting with something on the floor with my right foot, completely unaware. Lance notices. He looks at me in complete shock and I'm baffled as to why.

He asks, with uncertainty in his voice, "Are those his drawls?!"

I look down and calmly answer, "No, of course not. They're yours." In my mind they are Lance's.

Lance then proceeds to pick up the gray boxers as he yells, "I don't own any underwear that even resembles these." I curse out Kevin disordered, careless-self out in my head. Lance is going off and all I can think of is "How the heck you grab everything but your underwear? THEN leave them in plain sight, like you had to step over them at least 2-3 times. You had ONE job bruh." I immediately break down in tears because I failed; mission aborted. It was over. I was so close, oh so close to escaping what I was trying to avoid and what was surely to come. As I'm sitting in my feelings Lance has gone on a rampage and turned into the Tazmanian Devil. He has broken the mirrors that dually serve as sliding doors for my closet, the blinds in the living room that were concealing the balcony are now ripped down, eggs decorate the kitchen and living room walls and electronics are flipped over.

Lance leaves in a rage after dissembling the apartment. I receive a phone call shortly afterward from Lance's dad telling me that Lance is headed to find Kevin and he was going for blood. He asks me what happened but I could not bring myself to say I cheated so I just cry... CJ beeps in so I click over. The first words out of CJ's mouth are "You know you've done f***** up right? This boy is at the house where y'all had that house party and he's tearing s*** up! He done kicked the people cars, denting up s***. Cursing everyone out looking for Kevin." I get off the phone with CJ and send a text to Kevin apologizing for the chaos. He responds back ensuring me that it was all good and not to worry about it. In my head, I'm thinking, "You don't know Lance." I try to reach Liyah but there was no answer. I turn off my phone and bury myself in my bed.

I awake to much calmer knocks on the door. It's Lance and it is dark outside. He asks if he can come in, so I move to the side allowing him to walk in. He tells me he had my phone cut off after seeing text messages to Kevin. I inform him I had apologized for the way he was acting at his homeboy's house. Lance was, of course, not trying to hear any of it. After going back and forth I remind him that he came for a reason. He then tells me he came over as he wanted to come clean. He starts off with "CJ told me not to tell you but I've cheated too." Deep down I knew he had been cheating. His behavior was different. As of late, his appearances to my apartment would show up later and later and were dwindling down but I could never prove he was cheating even with that one text. I was hurt at the confirmation of my suspicion but to say I was shocked would be a lie. The icing on the cake, however, was the number of people Lance had cheated on me with and the length of time was a punch to the gut. He had slept with almost ten times as many people as I had. With no emotions I immediately ask for names,. He only gives me a handful of names but one name, in particular, set me off. Eboni. Maybe you recall my statement, "that's a story for another time?" Well, the time has come.

Eboni, "the Civilian", was a part of a student organization with me. We both were executive board members so we met frequently to plan events, discuss next outings, budget, etc. As time went on Eboni would confide in me concerning her boyfriend. I would give her advice just for her to return with another sad story of her boyfriend's disloyalty. At one point her boyfriend even tried to talk to me but I shot him down. I told Eboni it would be best for her to move on from him. Time passes and eventually, they broke up. Eboni and I would run into each other at parties and around campus; we always greeted each other with smiles, hugs and friendly convo. As I sit listening to Lance, Eboni's name struck a nerve. It hit deep. Sure, we were not the best of friends but she knew me and confided in me at one point or another. I ask Lance if her best friend knew as I was running down the list of people whose loyalty was suspect, to me from the news. He ensures me that she didn't know.

I'm running a timeline in my head trying to figure out when all this could have occurred. I'm thinking to myself, "how did I get myself involved in this bs?" I ask Lance how long has he been cheating. He doesn't answer, he just sits quietly. I ask again but this time anger is in my voice, "HOW LONG!" He lets out a whisper of the word "three." I do the math and he means "three" as in three whole years. I'm so upset at the answer I tell him to leave. I'm not sure if I was mad that our relationship was full of lies or the fact that I had cheated for a few months in comparison to his few years. He wants to continue to talk despite my request but I get up and leave. I have to attempt to clear my mind. Sort my feelings. Figure out if this was worth salvaging or abandoning. While attempting to figure things out I become heartless, numb. I no longer care for the well-being of Lance but instead resent him. I want revenge. "How dare he come for my neck when he had been cheating for years?!" I ask myself. All the days that made up those last three years played back: nights I spent waiting for him to return, nights I slept alone, crying, feeling unloved, abandoned and ultimately used. I'm outraged.

Lance is persistent and adamant about trying to make it work. I have no interest and tell him so. He presses the issue regardless. I'm emotionless but decide I could play a role in order to satisfy myself with retaliation. He suggests we go to couple counseling, which he offers to pay for. The sessions were useless. We argued and refused to see anything but the pain caused by each other's actions. Yeah, we accepted full responsibility for the acts we each committed but I was not willing to hop back into a relationship until I rectified my hurt. I was gung-ho on being an enforcer of the Golden Rule. So I decided to be friends with benefits with Lance, in my mind, but he was under the false impression we were beginning to work it out.

Chapter 8:
Knuck If You Buck

Zoe: "Get your ahh up! You're coming to this pool party tonight!"

Me: What pool party?

Zoe: Freak at the Creek. I just heard about it BUT it suppose to be lit.

Me: Oh yeah, I heard about it *wipes the sleep from eyes* Is that tonight?

Zoe: Hell yes! So come on and get ready because I have to go get Kelz and make an alcohol run.

Me: Aite. Give me a second. I was knocked out.

Zoe: Yes, bish! I know, that's why I came over.

Once I finish showering I throw on a black bikini, jean shorts, yellow loose-fitting tank top and sandals. We head out in Zoe's dark blue corolla to start our alcohol run, stopping at our favorite convenience store. I purchase two four loko's and Zoe buys armfuls of bootleggers. Our next stop is the ABC store where we buy two bottles of white and one bottle of fireball. The last stop, picking up Kelz. Kelz comes out sporting poetic justice braids and a cut up shirt and athletic shorts. She pulls out a blunt that puts the Corolla on ten. We pull up at The Creek, Zoe's apartment complex, and head to her apartment. While we are preparing the pregame our teammates start filing in with bottles in hands.

The music is bumping and bottles are on deck. I have a nice little buzz going. We all decide to head out to see if the pool party is live. To our surprise, the clubhouse is packed. The pool area is maxed out. Its dark out but the fluorescent necklaces and bracelets provided by the hosts had the place resembling a club. The pool area was gated in and we've heard, by word of mouth, the party was at maximum capacity. My teammates and I decide to hop the gate. One of our jumpers provides everyone a boost over the tall steel black gate, including random civilians. Once we were all inside we make our way to the pool enjoying the party. With red cups in everyone's hand, the dj has us vibing. Turns out the rumors were true it was lit.

We were partying hard, until all of a sudden, my friends all go quiet. Liyah tells me not to turn around but of course, what do I do? I turn around and see Eboni. I blank. I don't even remember getting out of the pool but somehow I'm mushing Eboni's face with the strength of Harambe (RIP). I'm yoked up by Lawrence, my teammate who was helping everyone hop the fence earlier. Still spazzing, I'm free and I'm back sprinting towards Eboni. There's a crowd, police and a double-overed Lawrence; I unknowingly kicked him in his nether regions amid my containment. Police are right around the entryway attempting to

44

close down the party as it has become out of hand exceeding capacity. I searched for Eboni but she was nowhere to be found.

My friends grab me in an attempt to calm me down and talk some sense into me as the cops are present but unable to see the commotion due to the crowd. Aaron walks up to me laughing with his hand out expecting me to dap him up as the crowd disperses. He proceeds "Yooo...Fight Night! I didn't know you had that in you." I'm still heated and not in the mood for jokes. I am pulled towards the parking lot where my ride was waiting. Everyone is staring as my friends are amping and replaying what just went down. It's loud and people are everywhere but I manage to hear "Aye, you good?" I look and it's DeShawn. I crack a smile, nod and get into Zoe's car. Zoe, our driver, is higher than a kite and has no idea of the events that just went down. She and Kelz have been in the car for a while now. Our teammates fill her in and she passes the blunt to me, "here, you need this more than me." She follows up with "You beat her a** right?!" I dully reply, "Not like I wanted."

Zoe: "Forget that b****. I seen DeShawn talking to you. What was that about?"

Me: Nothing. He just asked if I was okay.

Zoe: Mmhmm. Whelp! McDonald's run! *Pulls off with the speed of the Fast & the Furious*

Chapter 9:
Jupiter Love

About 1.5 months have passed since Freak at the Creek. I'm not going to front; I was still heated from the whole cheating debacle. While I do understand I am not without fault, I also was not with that many people nor for that length of time. Who am I to compare when we are both at fault? After all the events transpired, I felt the need to continue to satisfy my sexual desires also evening the score. For the most part, I kept my sexcapades to myself. The following summer after everything hit the fan, I began communicating with a guy named Bryce. Bryce is a very humble and intelligent young man who knows how to make everyone laugh. He was a big-time track and field athlete. He was from Ohio but went to school in Texas where he left his mark and launched his track and field career; he eventually ended up going pro.

We met via a live chat during a live stream of NCAA nationals. We were discussing track, of course, and the rest wrote itself. After multiple conversations, Call of Duty game sessions and Skype calls; he decided he would come to see me. I don't object to the request but I inform him that I do not want a relationship with him. Initially, he was down with the proposal of strictly being friends but things begin to change. One evening we decided to share intimate songs that gets us in the mood, some that made the list were: *Skin, Jupiter Love, All the Places* to name a few. I decided to compile the songs we listed and create a playlist for us just in case he ever came to visit. I never told him about the playlist.

The night Bryce shows up I am intoxicated with my usual group of friends, my teammates. We are heading to a house party in Zoe's neighborhood so we pre-gamed at Zoe's then walked to the party. We are walking and conversing, enjoying the surprisingly cool summer night when I receive a phone call from Bryce. He informs me he is in Athens, then inquires about my whereabouts. I try to compose myself, which is becoming difficult, considering that I am heavily under the influence. I reveal my location and try to separate myself from the group to meet up with Bryce, a person I have yet to meet in person.

I'm almost in the clear but Olivia turns and follows me yelling "Kendall! Wait up! Where are you headed?" I'm trying to quickly compose an excuse, a quick believable lie, but nothing comes to mind. I'm a horrible liar.

I smile as I tell her "I'm meeting up with an old friend."

She asks, "Do I know this friend? Is this friend a male?"

She is genuinely concerned but I roll my eyes due to the current inconvenience.

"Olivia, they're waiting for me. I'll find you and fill you in later. If you need me I'll be at Zoe's spot."

She gives me a side-eye, "Well if I don't hear from you in a reasonable time I'm coming to look for you."

I sarcastically answer, "Yes, mother. Bye!"

As I walk around the building I'm caught by surprise as Bryce is walking up the back steps of the passway between Zoe's apartment and a neighboring apartment building. "Sheesh, he was a lot closer than I anticipated" I thought. I'm immediately greeted with a hug and the most gorgeous smile. I melt in his embrace, he feels so good. I hurriedly instruct him to follow me as I do not have time to be spotted by one of Lance's informants. We make our way up two flights of steps making small talk. We enter Zoe's darkened apartment and head straight to Zoe's room. I'm starting to feel wrong for the foolishness that is about to go down; I don't want to add Zoe's bed to the messy mix; that's just disrespectful. I felt guilt for letting this go so far. Something that stemmed from innocent flirting led to me adding another body to my list. I was too far in to turn back now, the boulder was already in motion but I also was not sold on wanting to stop it. I lay down on Zoe's floor as Bryce kneels down on the floor with me while he undoes his jeans. I watch him get undressed as the street light shines through Zoe's blinds, providing just enough light for me to gaze at this beautiful man get undressed. The way he looks at me while he removes his jeans has me burning with desire and/or lust (take your pick). I become mesmerized by all the tattoos; he had informed me before that he had 72 tattoos in total but looking at them in person was a sight to be seen. He adorns a wonderfully painted mural on his upper body, a Picasso of the sort. The foreplay goes on and on -in my Erykah Badu's voice- which makes me antsier by the second, I feel like I can no longer handle the anticipation. I pull Bryce up and whisper in his ear "I want you inside me." He switches gears real quick and we are both on our way to the finish line when the condom pops, throwing us both off. Unfortunately for him, he does not have an extra and there is no way I am letting him back in without one. I am not on birth control nor did I want to catch anything. I start to get dressed as he sits, baffled. I tell him "maybe next time" as I finish throwing on the last article of clothing. I escort him out of Zoe's apartment as he is still throwing on his shirt. After I close the front door, I turn and give him a hug saying, "see you when I see you" then made my way back to my crew.

Chapter 10:
Birthday Chick

A few months later, on my birthday, in fact, TU is playing against the number one team in the nation. I have my birthday all planned out: we would go paintballing, go-karting, lunch then catch the big game. Liyah, her boo, some of our teammates and, also to my surprise, Lance all came to celebrate my birthday. After the activities we head downtown to discuss the game over burgers and fries. I check my messages and notice some of the football players sent me Happy Birthday messages. I thank them and take the opportunity to ask them to add a few people to their will call if it was not too late. They make it work allowing Liyah and Charity to join me at the game. The game is epic; keeping everyone on the edge of their seats. Some fans are on the brink of a nervous breakdown while others are celebrating by jumping up and down and high-fiving other fans after a clutch play. This is the best football game I have ever attended and I am a faithful fan if I do say so myself.

After the game, Liyah and I decide to go downtown since our school had just upset the number one team in the nation. We dawdle through the overly crowded streets of downtown. We somehow manage to hear our names being called from across the way. We turn around and see Bianca and Nicole across the street waving us over to them. As we greet our teammates I'm showered with hugs and happy birthdays. Nicole invites Liyah and I to her boyfriend's, Brandon, spot as they decided to have a little gathering over there. Liyah and I pull up to Brandon's crib and upon our arrival are mason jars of moonshine on their dining table.

As I ponder the many different ways in which I could say "no" to the white lightning concoction, my thoughts are interrupted by Brandon handing me a jar, peer pressuring me into consuming this mixture that resembles rubbing alcohol. I try to talk my way out of it but they are not letting the birthday girl have her way this time. With uproarious cheering I reluctantly, shove the warm strong tasting liquid down my throat in a failed attempt to bypass the taste. The smell alone could get you buzzed. After a few more sips I pass the jar and excuse myself making my way upstairs to the restroom. As I'm walking up the stairs I can feel someone eyes on me. I hear Liyah laughingly holler, "Kendall, Deshawn is looking at your a**!" I turn around, halfway up the stairs, and see Deshawn dumbfounded feeling embarrassed. Liyah follows up Deshawn's look with, "well you were looking mad hard, all in her butt." I laugh it off and enter Brandon's bathroom where I start texting Tyson and Rob to congratulate them on the win in addition to thanking them for the last minute extra tickets. I make my way back downstairs to a floor full of people vibing, socializing, drinking and having a great time; high off tonight's outstanding victory. I receive a call from Tyson but the music is blasting so I make my way upstairs, the commotion downstairs is being drowned out as I reenter Brandon's darkened bathroom. As

I'm sitting on the toilet seat lid cover talking to Tyson, he tells me he wants to see me but I inform him I am kicking it with my girls tonight at some of his teammates' place. He wants to come through but is too wasted to drive. I lie and say that I will get with him later. Deshawn walks in and sits on the side of the garden-style bathtub. I look at him as I continue to wrap up my phone call with Tyson. Deshawn whispers "Oh, you cupcaking? You want me to leave?" I shake my head while simultaneously mouthing the word "no." I close the bathroom door just enough so the lock doesn't click while Deshawn patiently waits for me to finish the call. I hang up the phone and question DeShawn.

"To what do I owe this unexpected (thinks to self: but highly anticipated) visit?"

Deshawn: Just making sure you're alright. You were in here for a while.

I side-eye him, "well, I was on the phone, is there something else..?"

He answers, "Just came to talk."

"about what? Anything in particular? Have you heard anything about me by chance?" I questioned.

He looks at me and I almost faint. He look so good!

Deshawn: "Nah, why? Is there something I need to know? You messed with one of my teammates or something?"

"Did he see the name in my phone?" I think to myself.

"Really dude?" says the look I give him as I tilt my head in response

"Don't play me. I know you know about me and your roommate, Allen."

He scuffs, "Yeah, but yall just kissed, y'all didn't have sex."

I nod in agreeance, "True. Well then, on that note, no I have nothing to hide."

He laughs and pulls me to him. I straddle him without any hesitation.

I curiously ask "Why are you trying me now? You've known me going on five years."

He reservedly answers: "You never seemed interested. You would never speak, you would just walk by like you didn't see me."

He starts kissing me passionately. The moment was so wanted and welcoming a chick was about to slide them panties off right then and there until I remembered…I was on my period. Dang! I try to back off but with very little will power and effort, he came on stronger. Then I remove my lips from his and inform him "I can't. This isn't right." I go to open the door and he pulls me back. "No, please don't go. Stay just a little longer." I look at him discouragingly, "I really should be going." He takes my hand guiding it below. I was lusting for Deshawn bad! I got back on top and start kissing him again while he caresses me. He was palming my posterior and I was just wanting to give him my all. Then it hit me again. I hop off his lap and go to open the door and I hear his sexy southern voice, "well, can I get your number?" In my head, I'm thinking, "Oh heck yes," but I keep my outer calm appearance intact and enter my number in his phone and immediately exit the bathroom, leaving Deshawn and his "mans" on ten. I quickly say my goodbyes to everyone and hurry Liyah to the car in where I fill her in on what just went down.

An entire week went by before I heard from Deshawn again. When he finally reached out, I was excited, upset and perplexed all at the same time. Before I could ask what had taken him so long he told me he had lost my number and had to get it from a teammate of mine. I found out later that his story checked out. Unfortunately for him, I wasn't in town because I was attending Clark Atlanta's homecoming; however, he told me he would wait up for me. He asked that I call him just in case he fell asleep. With that said, I was too ready to get back to TU. This was the guy I've waited for since I step foot on campus but I was always too shy to speak to him, he made me nervous honestly. Crazy right? I know. When it was time for us to leave, I thankfully had driven my car, so I made it back to TU in record time. Deshawn kept his word and waited for me. He answers my call but I could tell he was on the brink of sleep. I politely tell him we can get up another time if he's too tired but secretly hoping he wouldn't renig on his invite. He assures me that he's okay so I make my way to his place once I drop off all my homegirls.

Once I arrive, I park about a half-block away with the intention of not being seen parking near his place. I don't want to run the risk of being labeled as a groupie nor do I want any parts of the drama associated with it. At the front door, I knock lightly in hopes to not awaken his housemates. A shirtless Deshawn answers the door wearing basketball shorts and a grin. He gives me a hug that I welcome with excitement. He closes the door behind us and I lead the way to his room while he follows closely behind. His room is the typical jock setup; the huge flatscreen displaying SportsCenter, a king-sized sleigh bed, a copious amount of football paraphernalia, honors, newspaper article clippings and various awards displayed throughout the room. I sit on his bed relishing the fact this is actually about to go down. He breaks my thought process by asking me what I wanted to watch on TV. I reply, "SportsCenter is fine." He smiles, "Yeah, that's right. You're into sports."

He flips through channels for a few moments before getting up to insert a DVD into his PS4. Love and Basketball's title page appears on the screen and I look at him in slightly suppressed amazement as I ask "Did you know this is my favorite movie ever?" He replies, "Maybe." I mean I was already down, but the whole favorite movie fiasco made it a go. We didn't even

54

make it past the opening credits before I'm in my birthday suit. He proceeds without a condom but I stop him and inform him that I'm not on birth control nor was I trying to be anyone's mother right now. Deshawn had a very nice physique, smooth chocolate skin with a fine grade of hair. I love a fresh cut on a man. But Deshawn suddenly comes and comes hard. I hop off of Deshawn and proceed to throw on my clothes .He looks at me and said "D***..." with an undertone of disbelief. I say nothing but smile knowing I put it down, exceeding his expectations. He gets up and enters the bathroom to clean up. Upon his return, I am fully dressed and grabbing my keys. Deshawn states, "I expected it to be good but d***... I never had nothing like that before. That's a first." I chuckle and say "it only gets better" as I walk towards his bedroom door.

He stops me, "Wait, let me walk you to your car."

I reluctantly tell him, "I'm good" not wanting to appear attached nor needy. Despite my no he throws on some basketball shorts and asserts that he at least walks me to the door. As I walk down the steps, I could feel him staring at me. It was an oh so familiar feeling. At the front door, he hugs me and tell me that we'll keep in touch. I look up at him mid embrace and whisper "I'm sure."

From there, Deshawn and I have sex sporadically the next few months. I start becoming more comfortable with Deshawn, which is likely denoted by me choosing to leave immediately after every encounter. I guess I was afraid of rejection; I was afraid of him potentially telling me he wasn't really into me. While all this was going on I also was attempting to see where things were going with Lance and I. I decide to plan a vacation for Lance and I to see if we can amend what is left of our mangled relationship. Before I left for the trip, I call it off with Deshawn, informing him I'm working things out with Lance. Even still, we mess around one more time to end on a good note.

Chapter 11:
Unfaithful

I return, from Deshawn's place to my apartment where my roommate is chilling on the couch, watching TV. I sink into the loveseat adjacent to her and start to explain what I just did and who. Lance is at the gym playing basketball so I had no concerns about him questioning my whereabouts. I tell Sierra of the stunt I just pulled and immediately after my confession "*Unfaithful*" by Rihanna plays from my phone. I start to sing the song passionately as the words are hitting home. I look at Sierra who is singing along too but as soon as we made eye contact it dawns on us and we instantly burst out laughing, tears streaming down our faces at the timing of the song. Time goes even further to outdo itself as Lance walks through the front door.

The following morning, Lance and I have sex, great sex. Our sex was so great he forgets to pull out. For some idiotic reason, I thought the previous Plan B would still be lingering around in my system playing defense, therefore, I did not take any action. About three weeks later we are on our trip to Cancun. We have an awesome time and everything appears to be going fine. My period hasn't shown. I figure the period app I utilize has glitched but just to be on the safe side I purchase a pregnancy test.

Behold. I'm staring at a positive stick. I am shocked and pregnant. I don't know what to do, who to tell, my mind is everywhere but more so: Who is the father? Lance or Deshawn? My money is on Lance seeing how he had been raw-dogging me for the past four years but the last time I had sex with Deshawn he got some strokes in before I realized he was not wearing a condom. I am so nervous. I decide to tell Lance and leave Deshawn out of the picture. Having Deshawn in the whole ordeal would be too much. Lance did not know Deshawn and I messed around. I chose to tell Lance only because the odds were likely in his favor. He does not second guess if it was his or not. He goes straight to "we have to have an abortion." I am deeply hurt. Not so much that he did not want to have a child with me but that he is willing to kill one. I know I can say no and stand my ground but I am on the fence myself. I told myself beforehand that I would go with whatever he decided. I did not take into account that he would prefer an abortion.

There were protestors outside when we arrived. "I was once pro-life too," I thought to myself, "When did I suddenly decide I'm not?" I learned a valuable lesson. You truly do not know what decisions you'll make until you're actually in that situation. Once I found out I was pregnant I felt nervous, scared and alone. I've come to learn that feelings are not facts. They're fickle and will change on you. Unfortunately, I made decisions based on feelings. I did not want to tell anyone, not even my best friend Liyah as I felt ashamed and did not want anyone to know. She was secretly hoping that I would wind up pregnant; occasionally making jokes saying "So when you're pregnant, who's going to be the baby's daddy?" I never thought it would come to past. After taking multiple pregnancy tests, I thought of all the people whom I would have to tell and potentially let down. I would be having a child out of wedlock. Of course, having sex out of marriage is wrong, but that is something you can hide behind closed doors. All of that different from having a child. I felt my dirty laundry went public and was bound to make headlines, at least the TTOC.

I was afraid of the judgments, ridicule and backlash that was sure to come. I was scared and anxious about something that had not yet happened. I was afraid of the future I would not be able to provide for a child when I was just a college student in a rocky unstable relationship. I started to talk myself out of becoming a mother re-ensuring myself I wasn't ready financially nor mentally, so I sided with Lance but was still experiencing hurt and guilt. I felt Lance let me down. I felt pain from Lance's quick response as he had no hesitation with his answer; no noticeable remorse of the loss of innocent life. I was looking to him to say otherwise; to give me some sort of hope or strength that I could do it. It never came. Here we are sitting in the parking lot of a riotous pro-life group gathered around the premises.

As I walk inside the entire moment is feeling unreal; like a movie scene of someone's life but not mine. It felt out of place. I wasn't supposed to be here. I'm handed a clipboard which I take back to a vacant seat and begin filling out the required paperwork. Lance sits beside me in the waiting area as time slowly, painfully passes by, hearing names called one-by-one, just waiting in silence with the remainder of people, silent. I look around and see unhappiness, broken love and abandonment in the faces of some lone women. My heart ached for them, especially for the women who were there alone. I suddenly hear my name called and was asked to follow a nurse who was waiting for me at the door. I was taken back to a room that was rather dark and was instructed to lie on the table. They performed an ultrasound to confirm the pregnancy and then took me to another room. Once called upon, I was asked if I was here for: the oral (pill) or surgical procedure. I went with the oral option as I felt it was less invasive and less traumatic as I was only a couple weeks along. I was then instructed to sit in another waiting area. This newer lobby area was even more depressing than the previous. A sappy chick flick was playing on the TVs located on both ends of the room. No one was paying attention to the movie. My conscience would not let me. There was no chit chat of any sort. The only people you could hear were the pro-life protestors outside. Every so often a nurse would come in and call for the next patient to have her procedure carried out. Once my name was called, things started to go in slow motion for me. I felt light-headed but somehow managed to not faint. I was provided a small manila envelope, which could hold a key at most, but contained the pills that would carry out the elimination process with simple instructions stapled to it. I exited into the main lobby where Lance was still waiting. His presence made me feel a little better but not enough. We rode back in silence. He dropped me off at my home then pulled off to go back to his hometown. He informed me he had prior engagements with his family; therefore, I was left by my lonesome in my apartment to bear the pain, emotionally and physically.

After taking the abortion pills accompanied by pain killers, I was awakened from my sleep in the middle of the night with excruciating pain located in my abdomen. Had I not done research on the side effects beforehand I would have called 911. As I waited for the pain to subside, I sat on my toilet and cried. I cried from the pain as well as feelings of failure, abandonment and remorse.

Chapter 12:
Never Told

I never told Deshawn about the pregnancy or abortion. He stopped texting me after I called it off with him so I didn't feel comfortable bringing it up to him at this point. Deshawn entered the NFL draft and was drafted by the Ravens in the second round. He left before I could say goodbye. I did feel away about the way we stopped communicating but there wasn't really anything to be done about it.

The next summer there was a huge pool party at Zoey's apartment complex. It was the annual Freak at the Creek night pool party. I wasn't really up for attending this year. This was the same venue in which I was about to catch a charge. As for Eboni, "the Civilian", I apologized for laying hands on her. We had a heart to heart and decided to let bygones be bygones. I was over it. While recalling the events that had gone down that night I also remembered Deshawn checking on me in the parking lot, just ensuring I was good. To be fair, this was before my birthday incident and before I had started sleeping with him. I believe his concerns were truly genuine at the time. Like I said before, he's a gentleman. My feelings for him were surfacing with all the memories flooding in. I was not ready to face Deshawn after all this time while toting untold secrets.

Before we made our way to the pool, we went to meet Nicole. She was at Brandon's spot, Deshawn's former housemate. Bianca and I were thoroughly pregamed. We were roughly 90 feet from Brandon and Deshawn's spot when we see a group of guys, around 18 of them, walking our way. I try to quickly sober up just in case they're cute because no one likes a sloppy drunk girl. As we get closer, I spot Deshawn and I get all giddy on the inside. I manage to maintain my composure but I am experiencing butterflies. Bianca notices one of her other friends, Aaron, another one of Deshawn's former housemates along with Brandon and Allen. Bianca and I play it cool as we're approached by the group.

"What yall doing over here?" Brandon asks.

Bianca reply "We came to meet your girl."

I decided to walk off towards the house while Bianca replies as it was becoming unbearably awkward for me but Deshawn comes after me.

"Wait. Wait. Wait… You're not going to speak?" He looks at me with a puzzled, yet hurt look.

I look down because he made me feel bad. I knew I was in the wrong but I didn't know how to face him after all this time. I felt we had left off with unfinished business and I didn't know how to rectify it. I didn't know if he wanted to talk or would even be willing to talk now that he was playing for the Ravens. After all, I was the one who had left to fix damaged goods; he didn't owe me anything. I stammered, "I apologize, you just caught me off guard. I wasn't anticipating seeing you."

He leans in to give me a hug and Bianca nudges me implying we have to go. I leave with her and I could feel Deshawn just standing there, staring… most likely at my butt. I turn around and sure enough, I was right. He was just standing there sexy as ever, just smiling. I chuckle as I thought to myself "I still got it."

Chapter 13:
Let This Go

A few months later into the fall, Lance and I figured we needed some new scenery, a fresh start so we packed up our things and moved out of state. We landed in Charlotte, NC where he had a coaching job lined up and I found a job working at a rehabilitation center. Everything appeared to be going smoothly. Date nights, work social events and homemade dinners became the norm. We were two kids playing "house".

One weekend Lance decided he would return home, back in Georgia, to visit his family. I didn't mind some alone time so I thought nothing of it. While watching TV I pick up Lance's iPad that he left behind to dabble in some candy crush. While smashing colorfully wrapped candy and leveling up, an iMessage appears that is hovering over my current game. I read the message and the words on the screen instantly caused me to transform into a detective.

The message displays no name but the sender is acquiring Lance to come over. Considering the time of night, I knew where this was leading. I let the messages continue to roll through without me intervening. I'm unable to see Lance's replies, only the sender who is clearly a female ready to expose her all (physically that is). From my point of view, Lance went to homegirl's spot; and he took her up on her offer for all I know. At that moment, I felt completely foolish that I tried to make this work. Just when I thought he turned a new leaf, here I was sitting on a couch mad and betrayed yet again. I'm steaming and annoyed with myself. I decide to say nothing to Lance but play it cool until his return back to Charlotte.

Once he arrives after his trip, I distance myself, awaiting for him to confess his dirt, but I quickly become annoyed with his clueless antics. Being the person I am, I rip off the bandaid and bring up the messages. He makes up all of these stories about how his iPad had glitched stating he let a friend borrow it recently. I was over the lies. There was a minute part of me that wanted to buy into the lie; so I did my due diligence and researched apple malfunctions and did not come across a single troubleshooting comment, blog post, FAQ, etc. that even hinted towards the lie he constructed, nada.

I ask to see his phone, in which all evidence was deleted prior, but a new issue arose. He had an app titled "Tinder" on his phone. Not only was there one female but a whole app full of them. He tells me it's nothing serious and how he just likes to flirt, to see if he still has it. I want to leave, walk out at that very moment, but I let my thoughts get the best of me and overrule my instincts. I start to think about my funds, housing situation and how everything would solely be on me. I knew my current job was not going to sustain my lifestyle. I should have left then but I didn't out of fear of what I did not have, fear is just **F**alse **E**vidence **A**ppearing **R**eal but it felt very real at that moment.

Even though I ended up dropping the matter, I never truly forgot it. We continued to sleep in the same bed but sex was a no-go. I always made up an excuse or would sleep on the couch when I really didn't want to go through the motions of making up a lie. The piece of floss-like string that was holding our relationship together had unraveled. It appeared that we were not going to make it to the finish line after all, at least not together.

Chapter 14:
Own It

A couple of months have passed since learning of Lance's betrayal and I have started focusing on traveling more just to get a break from reality. Traveling had become my drug, my coping mechanism. Liyah asked if I would like to take a trip with her, Tokyo and Mya to visit Bo. Tokyo had prior obligations but Mya and I confirmed the visit.

You're probably wondering who Bo is; well, let me catch you up right quick. Liyah introduced me to Bo, who was an old high school friend of hers. Unlike myself, Liyah kept in close contact with her high school friends throughout undergrad. Bo went to college in Michigan so we didn't see him often. I met him a few times at house parties during the summer when he would return home to Georgia. It just so happened he would be out with his homies from high school who were also Liayh's high school classmates. Since then, they have all kept in touch. Bo had the potential to be a real gentleman but he was such a clown. For the record, potential should not be your guide. You can often see the product of what a man will be based around the company he most often keeps. With that being said, there were a few guys he hung around with, in my eyes, who was not very respectful to women, but that is a discussion for another day.

One week during the football season, Liyah, a few girls and I planned a trip to watch Bo play at Michigan since they were playing TU. The plans fell through. I forgot to mention how negligent Bo is at communication and following through. Bo ended up going pro and played for the Seahawks. Once he got settled in he invited us out to Seattle. Based on his less than stellar communication habits, we assumed he would flake on us again so we were somewhat hesitant but we okayed the trip and booked our flights. Before we knew it, we were on our way to Seattle.

Once we landed in Seattle, we were greeted by Bo and his handsome teammate. Liyah was very attracted to the new guy so she hopped in the front seat with him fairly quickly. Bo's car was a two-seater, sports car. With that said, he only had room for one of which Mya took dibs on, leaving me to climb in the back of the jeep with the cute roomie. We drove around 15-20 minutes as Bo and his teammate raced back to their place, recklessly weaving in and out traffic on the interstate.

We all make it to their spot in one piece. Upon our entry, Bo starts dishing out shot glasses. I figured I could use a shot to alleviate the stress of the airline losing my bag. Eric, Bo's fine housemate, informs us that he had to run back to the airport to pick up a friend. I ask him if he could check to see if my luggage had arrived as I was informed it was on a later flight.

While Eric makes his way to the airport, Bo, Mya, Liyah and I catch up on what's new then they reminisce on high school memories. While sharing laughs and swapping stories Eric walks in with another woman. Imagine our surprise as we were all under the impression it was going to be a male friend. While everyone was surprised at Eric's additional guest, I was ecstatic as Eric was able to retrieve my bag. I thank Eric and he introduces the new girl as Amber. We all greet her and discuss the move for the night. Bo and Eric suggest we all go out. They call a driver who arrives in a spacious all-black stretched Escalade, fully stocked with copious amounts of alcohol. Upon arrival to the club we are provided red carpet treatment and escorted to an upper-level VIP section where some of their teammates were being served by bottle girls. Strobe lights illuminated the packed dance floor while the DJ mixed all the latest hits. We're on an upper level in which I noticed some of their teammates are here. We're introduced but I barely catch names as the music is drowning out their voices. I smile and nod my head in the hopes they believe I got everything they were saying. I don't even remember how we got back as I awoke in the bed to a sleeping Liyah and a snoring Bo. The three of us were knocked out on his California King size bed, no one noticing the presence of the others. And no, nothing happened.

As everyone starts to awake, we plan the activities for the day. Bo informs us that we could all grab breakfast together but he and Eric would be at team activities for the majority of the day. We all grab breakfast, the six of us, plus some guy I had no recollection of who crashed on the couch. As we all finish eating, each guy throw a card in a fitted cap and shake it up, mixing up the cards. Mya is given the honor to pull a card out of the hat therefore awarding the card owner the bill. Bo ended up being the lucky guy. We all thank Bo and climb into our respective vehicles. As I go to get in the back of Eric's jeep, Mya taps me on the shoulder and said "Bo asked if you want to ride with him?" I thought it was an odd request as I didn't know him as long or as well as Mya or Liyah but I didn't have any reservation about it neither.

Once back at the condominium, Eric pulls out a guitar. He strums his guitar as Amber sat beside him mesmerized. Bo, playfully throws something at me that grazes my head interrupting the concert that was commencing. I jump up which entices him to run. I start chasing him around the condo and I'm gaining on him. He feels the pressure of being caught. Right when I'm closing in on him he shuts a door behind him causing me to run into the door ricocheting to the floor. Everyone hollers in laughter at the scene. I laugh at myself as Bo opens the door extending a hand with tears streaming down his face from the aftermath. I'm fine but embarrassed. I hear my phone chime and it's DeShawn. Coincidentally Bo and Deshawn's teams were facing off this weekend. He asks if we all could get up but Bo and Eric are off to head to a team meeting. He understands and suggest meeting after the game.

The four of us girls spend the remainder of the day exploring the Seattle life, checking out the space needle, trying local eateries and, of course, shopping. After having dinner and getting to know Amber a little better we decided to stay in for the night. The guys are not returning tonight as game day is tomorrow; so we decided to have a girls' night. We occupy the night with relationship talk, or lack thereof with snacks and wine.

The next morning we awakened to the sound of Bo grabbing clothes from his closet and asking "which look better?" I make my selections out of the options provided to me. He inquires if we had any Seahawks apparel to wear. Even though I did the rest of my friends did not. He gives me the money for us to find Seahawks game wear. He informs us that Amber has our wristbands and that our driver would arrive later to take us to find some clothes. He's in a rush to head back but further delays himself by busting jokes. We inform him that he needs to leave and he agrees, finally. We wish him good luck as he heads out the door.

Amber is pouring shots for everyone to take as I'm wiping my eyes, it's still pretty early and my body has not fully adjusted to the time difference. She hands out double shot glasses and said, "It's Game Day Ladies!" We clink our glasses and throw them back. "I don't think I have ever had a shot this early," Liyah expressed. We laugh and Amber turns on some music. We get dressed while intermittently gathering to take shots in various stages. We figured we should grab something to eat as it is still considered breakfast time, and if we were to keep this alcohol consumption rate up we needed something other than alcohol in our stomachs. Amber suggested a restaurant that served brunch that was in walking distance so we decided to make the short walk. While enjoying our selections, Amber is telling us stories of how her and Eric met and how often she visits.

After heading back from brunch, we take a couple more shots. Mya informs us the driver is downstairs. We make our way into the all-black stretched limo with tinted windows. We make enough stops that everyone finds what they wanted. After purchasing our items we head to the game in style with drinks, a constant theme this weekend. Amber distributes our bands and tickets informing us of the perks and amenities that come with the bands. We drive through waves of fans tailgating but decide we want in on the experience prompting us to ask the driver to stop so we can get out and partake in the festivities. He obliges, pulls over and let us out. The band is playing their theme song and fans are dancing, singing, laughing and just having a great time. I'm embracing the experience as this is my first time attending an NFL game. Amber leads us to our seats which are inside a luxury box. Our armbands privy us to drinks and food at the bar located directly behind our seating area.

The stadium starts to fill up while the opposing team takes the field to warm up. We see Bo, Eric and their teammates come onto the field and the fans cheer, as the anticipation of the game builds. After warmups, both teams head back to the locker room.

Fireworks and music roar signaling the commencement of the game; the crowd rival the thunderous commotion with cheering, whistling and clapping. As Eric and Bo make their separate entries onto the field we root from our box at the top of our lungs. Kickoff proceeds shortly afterward. The game starts off well but by half time Seattle is down by two touchdowns. We decide to grab some food and a few more drinks.

While awaiting my loaded nachos I receive a text from Bo "That joint is dope AF!" He was responding to a picture I sent him while I was crashing tailgates. The picture was of a fan that had a drawing on display of him. The convo did not last long I assume he went back to focusing on work. As they take the field, the girls and my eyes are glued to the field. On the opening play of the second half, a receiver of the Ravens catches a short pass, jukes Eric and breaks free awarding his team an additional six points. Seattle's defense was struggling to say the least and the offense did not look much better. We find ourselves looking disheveled, throwing our hands up at each unfortunate event; albeit turnover, sack, etc. Seattle got blown out but I notice Deshawn had a pretty good game as he manages to get in some big tackles. I shoot him a text to congratulate him on his performance. In his reply, he asks if I would meet him by their bus after the game. I kept my word and drag Liyah with me right before the game clock wind down to 00:00.

Liyah and I run off without informing Mya or Amber assuming Amber wouldn't be up for the trip and we didn't want to leave her by herself so we sacrificed Mya. In retrospect, I did not think it through at all. After multiple directions from stadium workers and security we finally make it to our destination. There is a barricade placed where friends and family gather. An officer is posted up to the side to ensure order. One of the mothers of the more famous players of Deshawn's team was standing beside Liyah and I. She turns to us and said, "Who you here for?" I answered her, "Deshawn." She said without any hesitation "Oh, I don't know that *ninja*" and turns back forward. Liyah and I are taken aback but are trying not to laugh. Her blunt dismissal of us came back around. While awaiting the players to come over to the area Ms. Important decides she would make her way out to the meeting area prior to instructions given by the officer, she was told to hold tight. Someone in the crowd states: "Aye, you know who that is? That's Steve's mom." In which the officer politely but firmly states "I know who she is. She gotta wait too!" with no hesitation. I look at Liyah and we burst out laughing amongst the hushed crowd at Ms. Important's humbling expense. I feel my phone vibrate. I notice a missed call and a text that read: "Where you at?" I try to wave him down as I see him attempting to call me again. I get his attention. He comes over and Liyah gives him a hug, then he hugs me, his embrace is still everything I remember. We discuss the game and he mentions how he knows Bo probably mad. I go "yeah...that was a rough game for them." As we're talking Mya is calling Liyah and I informing us that Eric is waiting on us. We feel bad as we know he is more than likely ready to just go home after that defeat. We tell Deshawn we have to go and start racing back towards the stadium.

We still don't know where we are to go, so we just start running nowhere fast. After various wrong turns and dead ends, we end up in a random parking lot in which we are instructed to just stay there until they pick us up. Eric pulls up in his jeep and we enter. It's so quiet. There's no music playing, no talking, zilch. A vast difference from what we just left, polar opposites. I try not to make eye contact with Liyah as it's taking everything in me not to laugh. I can feel her staring at me and my eyes begin to water from containing my laughter. We understood the tone but we laugh at inappropriate times. Seated in the back seat, we felt like two bad kids who just got in trouble. As Eric begins to pull off, fans gather around the driver's side of his car asking for autographs. He signs 4-5 autographs and then another guy requests a pic. Eric obliges but the guy somehow messes up the first one and asks for another as Eric was preparing to pull off.

The fan goes, "Wait. Wait. One more I messed up." In which Eric sternly replies with some base in his voice, "Man, get that s*** right!" Now I'm about to lose it. I want to scream with laughter. Tears stream down my face but I don't make a sound. Fans are mobbing around the car in which someone asks Eric for a shoe. Eric states, "I got to go" and pulls off.

Now let me break down the sitting arrangement, Amber is sitting in the front, Mya is behind Eric, Liyah in the middle and I'm on the right sitting behind Amber. There is still silence until the silence is awkwardly broken with a phone call from Jess, Eric's ex. We know this is his ex as her name was indeed brought up during our girl's night. Now the call did not just ring from the phone, no it's connected to Bluetooth so it's coming from the Jeep's custom audio system. Eric presses ignore and the audio system loudly notifies us all "CALL IGNORED." The ex calls back again. He ignores it again and we are notified yet again, "CALL IGNORED." The hilarity increases between Liyah and I. We struggle to withhold our laughter. Mya, meanwhile, appears unamused. The kicker was when the ex called back a THIRD time in which the previous results carried out once more. By this time we have arrived to our destination. Liyah and I hop out the jeep so fast leaving Amber and Eric to discuss the stream of ignored phone calls and Mya nonchalantly followed behind us, unbothered. Liyah and I do not need to exchange words as we are both busting at the seams of laughter. Mya walks up and interjects, "Yall know y'all wrong." We continue to chuckle as Mya fobbed us into the elevator. We enter Eric and Bo's place and to our surprise, Bo is not present. The three of us take showers and start formulating dinner plans when Bo walks in as if he had not been MIA the past hour. All he said was "Aye, yall come with me. We going to my teammate's crib." Liyah and I follow him as he hypes up his teammate saying he's a cool dude and such. I guess Mya didn't get the memo as she was nowhere to be found on this voyage to the teammate's crib.

His teammate, Raymond, opens the door as music is drowning out any background conversation. Three girls are sitting on a couch as we pass by them heading into another room. In this room the lighting is red and chairs are arranged in a circle; Raymond starts grinding marijuana with a spice grinder. There are two other guys present, one of whom crashed on the couch the other night, he went by the name, Milk. These guys are high and laughing hysterically, we quickly realize where Bo has been the last hour and at this moment it makes sense why he was in such a jovial mood when he came to the front door. Liyah sits down with musical chairs energy, taking the last chair in the room. I'm lightly pulled by Bo, who is already sitting, as he guides me to sit on him. He is so big, I felt like a child sitting on one of his legs. The blunt makes its way to me. I hit and pass. Mid pass, I'm reminded of what Amber warned us about during our "girl talk": "They have this weed that makes you horny as s*** its called..." I blank on the name but see the blunt being passed back to me. I'm spacing out and laughing at the conversation even though I have no idea of the topic at hand. We're all laughing and unexplainable chipper. Abruptly we all become hungry and start to raid Raymond's cabinets. Liyah stuffs an Easy Mac cup under her Seahawks top. That makes me giggle when Bo spills purple and orange Nerds candy all over the floor. Someone tries to sweep up the nerds but is too high to work a broom properly. Raymond reiterates he is hungry, which prompts us to remember we were going to cook. In walks Mya, through the front door, jaw ajar at the scenery. Raymond pulls out shot glasses from a cabinet and starts pouring. Liyah and I agree to cook so we decided to head back at the moment Mya started looking for us. Amber informed Mya of our whereabouts and told Mya that she would come later on, which was code for "I'm not coming cause I'm still dealing with Eric." As Liyah proceeds to walk out, part of the Easy Mac cup peers out from her shirt. Raymond, feeling betrayed, asks "Yo, you were gonna steal my easy mac?" We all fall out laughing and head back to Bo's place to throw down on a southern home-cooked meal but we just could not get it together. We were complete giggle boxes. I go lay down on the bed in hopes that Liyah and Mya would cook. Bo comes in the room, closes the door behind him and starts to light candles. "Shoot, Amber forewarned us, and the weed still got the best of me," I thought to myself .

We were both enjoying the moment until I hear the words "I came." I hit a mini panic mode as I inform him I'm not on birth control and insist he finds a pharmacy open to purchase a Plan B. I was not going down that path again. While he's out driving to a pharmacy, guilt sinks in. I remember Liyah saying, "Yall going to end up having sex, watch." I recall this moment vividly as I was so adamant that she was wrong. Her intuition is shockingly accurate. I shower, get dressed in PJ's and walk to the kitchen to a smiling Liyah. I shake my head as Raymond walks in asking "Where's the food?" I respond, "My bad, another time. We got carried away." His face drops as he look mad hurt that we didn't cook. Then he starts singing "Own it" as he walks out the front door, Liyah bursts out laughing and I shoot her a shocked look inquiring, "He knows?!"

A few moments later, in walks Bo, as I'm lying in the bed wondering what's taking him so long for the errand. Bo states, "Every pharmacy I went to was out of it but I got one." I thank him, take the pill and go to sleep. We awake the next morning and pack our bags to head back home. Bo is knocked out and is barely awoke as he fumbles for his phone. He tells us our driver is downstairs and send us out with hugs. I had a long plane ride back to think about all that went down, to mull it all over.

Chapter 15:
Keep You in Mind

Bo and I periodically communicated but it was always small talk. He would randomly facetime me while I was at work or late at night so I didn't answer too often. I guess the change in time zone played a role but eventually the texts, convos, facetime calls all died out but someone else decided to resurface.

I'm now back in Georgia visiting some former teammates. We decided to have somewhat of a slumber party in which we had some cocktails, discussing our various relationship issues and playing games like truth or dare.

While in the middle of our festivities, I receive a text from Deshawn asking if I was in town. Although I missed his presence, I no longer wanted to be on demand for him. I hadn't really heard from him since the Seattle game which was months ago. I decide to ignore the text. Once the games and conversation started to die down, that text came back to mind. I finally reply back with "yes, are you?" Brandon text Nicole around the same time I receive a text containing Deshawn's new address. I hop in the shower and pack an overnight bag from my weekend bag. I throw my overnight bag in the passenger seat and make my way to Deshawn's place. Nicole and I pull up to the same place at the same, exact time. We laugh at each other parked beside one another, thinking the same thing. Nicole beats me inside as I take a few extra moments to ensure I'm looking right. I finally make it to the front door and one of his former college teammates, Allen, opens the door in Nike sweats and a white tee. With a warm greeting he whispers "Aye yo, you know you don't have to do this...Don't do this." This warning blindsided me. I wasn't in the right mindset to receive it. For a second I considered Allen's advice as he was genuinely looking out for me -hoping I would respect myself, carry myself as such and not go this route- but I wanted to, so I proceeded into enemy's territory. Deep down I knew he was right; just as I was ignoring my soul's red flags, I ignored him.

I find Deshawn's room and he's laid out on his bed tipsy. He states, "I've missed you" as he draws me in closer to him. I start to get undressed as he picks me up and places me on top. We do something that resembles two numbers transposed. I'm enjoying this short-lived moment. He falls asleep beside me as I think about my poor life choices thus far. As daybreak, I hurriedly get dressed and gather my items quietly, hoping not to awake Deshawn. As I'm half-way dressed Deshawn rolls over and asks, "What's the rush?" I inform him that I am meeting some friends to go wakeboarding. He follows up, "this early?" "Yeah and I can't be late" I respond. I tell him to hit me up later as I'm putting on my shoes. He asks "well you want something to drink?" I accept the offer, requesting water for the road. He brings me back bottled water while I ensure myself that I have placed all my items in my bag, including my feelings for him. He brings up the Seattle game and one topic leads to another. Next thing I know, I'm running late. I hug Deshawn and exit in a hurry before I become late.

I arrive at the dock in which I was the last to arrive. We all put on our life vests and climb into the boat. Mya receives a facetime from Bo inviting us to visit him in Pensacola. Of course, we're all down for a trip so we all confirm our attendance. We had a ball wakeboarding and memories were formed. On the ride back inland we discuss dates to visit Bo. We found a span that accommodated the majority, except Liyah, as she would be out of the country. The rest of us, however, were going to Pensacola in two weeks.

Two weeks pass and we are taking a road trip on our way to Pensacola. We're about 30-45 minutes out when Mya dials Bo on speakerphone: "Okay, we're not far out Bo. Don't have us locked out." Bo replies, "Yo, yall are not going to believe what I just did. I ran to the store and got a car full of groceries. Ran inside to get a cart and locked my d*** keys in the car. So I have a car that's running that's full of groceries."

Mya follows up in a dull tone, "Really, Bo?"

We pull up to the resort where we are granted a guest parking pass and then directed to Bo's condo. Upon our entry, we found Bo putting away groceries, after he managed to get into his car. Bo greets us all then cuts on music, asking each of us "brown or white?" I stuck with the majority choice, patron, despite the fact I don't enjoy tequila. We are all dancing, having a bootleg karaoke night. Mya performs sporting one of Bo's fitted caps backwards. Eventually, we all end up crashing after a heavy drinking-induced good time with a medley of song impersonations and off-key singing.

We all awake in the morning covered in white powder, because Bo decided to smack everyone with baby powder. Childish. Did I mention that Bo is a prankster? As we clean baby powder off our faces, he informs us that he has to go to the training room for rehab. "I'll be back for lunch," he yells as heads out the door. We spent the day by chilling out, watching tv, walking on the beach, and enjoying each other's company. The whole time I'm plotting how to get Bo back from the baby powder mayhem. I decide to use one of the oldest tricks in the book and wrap a hair tie around the kitchen sink faucet sprayer. I forewarn all the ladies as we sit in the living room and dining area, anticipating Bo's arrival. We finally hear him at the front door as we continue to "act normal."

While entering he asks "What y'all been into all day?" Nicole answers, "Just chilling, enjoying the beach." He replies, "Oh yeah, they have jet skis out here too, yall trying to go?" While, talking, he grabs a glass out of the cabinet and proceeds to rinse the glass. The anticipation is real as we are all awaiting this moment. As soon as he lifts the handle he gets hosed down. We explode with laughter while he is struggling to cut the water off. Bo's seizure like reaction while attempting to cut the water off is hilarious. We cried laughing. He goes "Alright. Yall got me, yall got me." Once everyone regained composure, Bo suggests we grab some food. It's an awkward time to go eat as its too late for lunch but not quite dinner but everyone is hungry regardless.

Bo wants to take us to a place he is very excited for. When we arrive, the line appears to be too long for how hungry we are. He options to take us to another place called *The Grand Marlin*. We're seated and I'm feeling underdressed in my beachwear. The place is more upscale than I anticipated but the waiting staff was accommodating regardless. Bo orders appetizers and signals the waiter to come closer. He whispers something that I am unable to make out. The waiter nods and returns with various appetizers and shots of brown for the ladies as we all wanted to be "surprised" from when Bo asked what we wanted to drink earlier. We toss back our shots before the waiter could leave. I guessed the name of the specific liquor. The waiter shocked, answers "yes." Bo jokingly calls me an alcoholic, I shrug it off and start to indulge in the appetizers. We chat amongst ourselves and plan the activities for the remainder of our visit. Our food comes out on cue. I am nearly full after killing the BBQ flavored oysters and fried lobster fingers. We called it a night in order to tackle the busy day ahead of us; Bo had tomorrow off so we were banking on making the most of it.

The next morning, Mya and I make breakfast for everyone: Wheat blueberry French toast, fresh fruit, bacon, and scrambled eggs with veggies and cheese. The aroma of brunch wafted through the condo enticing the others to get up. Once everyone ate and was fully dressed we all headed out to the beach. The vibrant rays from the sun beam off the teal waves that collide with the off-white powdery sand. Bo leads us to a Jet Ski rental that is conveniently a very short walk from the condo. He purchased everyone rentals as we teasingly chanted "He got moneeeyyyy". We paired up and had a ball, all taking turns operating the jet skis and riding with Bo. After we finish up we decide to go to the mall. I purchase a pair of Nikes as I didn't bring any sneakers, and we grab lunch at the food court. We spend time discussing the difference between the male and female thought process, double standards and 'what-if' scenarios. Bo was outnumbered when it came to differing gender perspectives but he held his own and it provided great entertainment none-the-less. Once we left the mall we did some sight-seeing driving along the coastline. Mya and others (mostly Mya) pressed Bo to invite some guys over. Bo reluctantly agrees to sets something up.

It's dark and everyone is hungry yet again. We make a food run and haul it all back to the condo. Our night was soon to begin. Music is booming in the condo, shots are being passed around and everyone is vibing. There's a knock at the door. Four big guys enter, all of which play football as well. One of them, we ran into the other day while he was walking his dog. We all introduce ourselves and one in particular immediately earned the name "Bruh man." I doubt he resided on the 5th floor but he was awarded the nickname due to his attire and stature. He entered in wearing a dark blue robe and slides. To entertain ourselves we, the adults, decided to play hide-n-seek, using all of our condos as a free-for-all and a neutral floor for the base. Bruh man ended up being the absolute worst at hiding, hiding behind curtains when you could clearly see his feet or other more obvious places to hide like behind a plant. In his defense, being 6'5 didn't leave him many options. After several rounds, we all ended up at Bo's condo. Two players dropped out due to early morning workouts and the rest of us decided to play truth or dare. The game became intense but it was so much fun.

Chapter 16:
On a Wave

My alarm goes off, it's still dark outside and my body does not want to fully awaken. I force myself out of the bed, sluggish in getting dressed. I grab my bag that I finished packing just hours before. I lock the door behind me and head towards the parking deck to retrieve my car. Still somewhat in a stupor I make my way on the interstate and head towards Virginia. I receive a good morning text as daylight is breaking through. I respond with "Good morning." I receive another text that reads "Are you on your way?" I reply "Yes, I'm an hour and 15 out." He texts back "Good, drive safe baby."

Upon arrival to the practice facility, I drive up a slight hill and pull up to a par-kut. I'm greeted by an older gentleman who politely tells me good morning and then asks for my name. In exchange for my name he hands me a parking pass and a VIP pass.

He provides instructions on where I could park and where to enter once parked. After parking I make my way to the practice field, surrounded by fans. One of the security guards grins as I walk around aimlessly. He waves me towards his direction where the players' families were located. I thank him and take a seat in the bleachers opposed to the tent and awning where majority of the family members, mostly wives, girlfriends, infants and toddlers, are seated. I presume these are nice ladies, however, I feel more comfortable sitting next to the youth team that was invited due to their great performance during their, I'm assuming, summer league. I'm not up for small talk and questions. I did not feel comfortable engaging with others as I did not have a title associated with Bruh man. We were going with the flow, but I had a general idea how that would come across.

As practice went on I notice more families coming closer to the bleachers. I go towards a tent where there is a smorgasbord consisting of hors d'oeuvre and little delicacies. The waiters and waitresses are dressed similar to those of a fine dining restaurant. I place a few items on a small silver saucer and make my way to the balcony to what looks like the "men only" club. All of the patrons were dressed in slacks with jackets discussing the season and future of the team. I listen but keep my thoughts to myself. I eavesdrop long enough to decide I want to head back to the bleachers where the youth team was sitting. By this time the practice session is wrapping up and some of the players make their way over to the perimeter of the field to sign autographs. The youth, sitting beside me, jump up to snag autographs and take selfies as practice ends. I sit in the stands for a little while before deciding to join the crowd. I didn't plan on getting autographs so I had nothing to hand the players but the "MVP pass" attached to my lanyard. I hand the pass to the head coach, starting QB and a LB. All three did a double-take on the item they are signing. I chuckle at their thought process then take a seat back in the bleachers. I receive a text from Bruh man asking where I was. I send him my location and he comes over to the side and brings me on the field. He asks if I am hungry. I respond, "I could eat." We make our way to another tent hidden on the backside of the practice facility. This tent accommodates the team's players, family, team workers and an abundant amount of food. The selections are delicious but I could not eat much due to the 'excitement' of it all. I kept my composure but I was truly impressed he invited me. Once we finished eating he rides with me back to their resort and hands me a key to his room. We chill, watching TV for a while before we hear a couple knocks on the door. It's a teammate and his wife whom he introduced me to. We chat for a while. They decide to go grab ice cream and invite us to accompany them on their ice cream run. Bruh man looks at me to provide a signal. I politely decline with "next time" as I'm still full from dinner earlier and also needing a nap. They tell us they will hold us to that as they exit the room. After they leave, we watch a show or five and talk about our last encounter. It's getting late and I'm still depleted from the drive. I start prepping for a shower by gathering my PJs and other items and placing them on the bed. While I'm getting ready for my nightly routine I hear him come from behind, suddenly feeling him hug me without saying a word. I turn around as he loosens his embrace and I sit on the bed. He kisses me and I'm teetering on the next move I should make. What should I do? This is our first time alone. Then I remember I'm on my cycle so I blurt out, "I can't, I'm on my period." He whispers in my ear, "Let's go to the shower." I was not anticipating that response. Talk about jumping the gun. That seems like a response of someone who has done it at least twenty times over, not someone going at it for the first time with one another. A part of me was hesitant but I made my way past the light green flowered wallpaper and entered into the bathroom threshold. He cuts the water on, extending his hand out. I take his hand and enter into the stream of warm water that is now beading on my front and trickling down my back. He starts to kiss me on my neck and caress me as the water flows over us, connecting us in a way that seems fitting, romantic even. After showering, I go to sleep with

Bruh man's arms wrapped around me feeling protected. I awake the next morning to a half-dressed man who looks at me while saying "good morning." He is getting dressed but apparently running late. He asks if he can take my car to rehab, I toss him the keys from the nightstand then roll back over to go back to sleep. He tells me he won't be long, because he was only going for treatment. His statement barely registers, to me, as I am not trying to jeopardize being fully awakened at this point.

When I finally awaken I hop in the shower and as I'm showering I hear him enter the room. "What do you want to eat?" I finish up my shower and grab a towel to dry off, I reply "something quick. I want to get back on the road before dark." He enters the bathroom as I'm now beginning to brush my teeth while adorning undergarments. He walks behind me whispers the words "Do you have to leave so soon?" I get weak in the knees and smile as I finish brushing my teeth. After rinsing my mouth with mouthwash I answer back, "yes, I do." He replies, "I know, I just wish you could stay longer." I sigh and turn to him "me too." He follows up with "then stay." I chuckle at the thought thinking "if only it was that easy." I walk out the bathroom and proceed to put on the remainder of my clothes while pondering the idea.

After we grab lunch I pack my items. I was determined to leave before dark. After failed attempts to convince me to stay longer I hit the road to return to reality, a messy life. A messy life in which I was still sharing living quarters with Lance.

Chapter 17:
Don't Think They Know

I returned back to Charlotte where Lance awaited. He asked about the yard sale back home. I recalled the lie I told him, which entailed me going back home to help with a yard sale. Sticking to my guns, I gave him a solid story about the imaginary yard sale. He didn't have a reason to second guess it so we carried on as before, living together but being apart. I no longer cared if Lance was trying to make it work or not, or even if he was entertaining someone else it did not matter to me. At this point, in my eyes, we were just house mates. I went to the movies by myself, shopping, eating, and checked out new places by my lonesome. I enjoyed it. A few months go by while I'm appreciating this adventure of life by myself. During this time I'm also entertaining conversations with various men that do not lead anywhere with the exception of one. The conversations with this guy were not daily but frequent enough to grab and keep my attention.

After a time, Lance and I decided it was best if we move on apart from each other. Our relationship had ran its course. He landed a new job which required him to move to another state. I had to move back home, with my mom as I didn't have the savings that would support me on such notice nor a well-paying job as I was looking to return back to school. As humbling as the situation was I figured moving back home would actually work in my favor for grad school, in-state tuition. I packed up all my things and left before Lance could say goodbye. Not sure he would have anyway as I didn't think he would care. We would engage with only the bare minimum of communication. Moving back home was indeed humbling and forced me to re-evaluate my life. I started attending church again and the sermons always hit home for me. I was realizing the life I was living wasn't my best. I was in deep like an addiction. I took a couple of small trips to visit my friends in Ft. Lauderdale and DC to help blow off some stress but they were only temporary fixes as I always returned back to the mess I had created.

In the midst of all this I kept in contact with Bruh man and a new guy that went by BZ who played for the Steelers. He was a cool, country guy during our phone calls and text chats but his social media personality was over-the-top, gaudy and scandalous. This was an unattractive trait to me so I chose not to entertain him as much. One day I received a text from Bruh man. By now, I do believe he has earned the right to be called by his actual name, Keenan. His text read: "Good morning! You was still trying to come to the game?" I read his text with excitement but respond with a basic "yup." He replies "Good, I got you a ticket. Are you able to get off work?"

"Sheesh, its last minute but I should be fine," I respond.

"Okay, good."

I swipe my inbox away returning to my home screen. I'm now excited; I get to attend my first home team game!

False Start: A Record of Experiences

The next day, I make my way to his hotel and pull into the parking deck. I send Keenan a text in which he instructs me which room to come to and how to get there. I text him to open the door. The door opens, he laughs mentioning it was unlocked as he leans forward to hug me. I give a shy smile welcoming his embrace. It's early afternoon and the game is scheduled for tomorrow evening. After he finishes getting dressed we walked around the area, passing small shops that are conveniently placed around the hotel. Catching up on each other's lives and reconnecting, reliving old events. Time passes til it is dark. We grab dinner to take back to the hotel.

After eating, I shower and throw on some shorts and a tank top to go to sleep. Keenan who was sitting on the bed now comes lie down behind me. He pulls my entire body towards him with his left arm in one swift effortless motion. I hear the oh so familiar, but appreciated, words "I miss you." I melt at the gesture as I start to feel soft kisses on the nape of my neck. I ensure he has a condom as I remind him I am not on birth control. He gets up and rummage hurriedly through a bag to obtain one. Once found, we pick up where we left off. It felt great but eerily wrong. I enjoyed it but my heart felt anguished. My upbringing of abstinence is resurfacing and tugging at my heart.

The next morning I awake to a gentle breeze coming from the balcony. He tells me he wants me to visit him in New York. I am flattered but on the fence about this tentative visit. I tell him I need time to think it over and blame it on work even though my work schedule was not the culprit. He replies, "I'll work around your schedule." The short phrase that left his mouth made me feel special, important to him. It was now time for him to leave in order to get ready for the game. He kisses me and tells me my ticket is at will call. He leaves me in the room on a high. I start to get ready for the game myself by throwing on my team jersey and gathering my items to place into my overnight bag. I leave the hotel and make my way to the stadium to catch my favorite team vs my favorite player and his squad.

Chapter 18:
Permission

I touchdown in JFK and call Keenan, "Hey, I'm here!"

"Cool, I'm about five minutes away," he tells me.

"Okay, no worries, I have to get my luggage." After grabbing my bags off the carousel, I make my way out of the exit doors and I'm greeted by a tinted black Rolls-Royce. Keenan steps out the driver's side to place my luggage in the back. As soon as I place my seatbelt on we're off and he's asking me if I'm hungry. I tell him "I could go for a bite to eat." He informs me that my plane landed too late to go to the Kevin Heart's standup but we would figure something out. After grabbing dinner we pull up to his place, a penthouse overlooking the skyline of NY. The city lights dance throughout the busy streets, reflecting off the various skyscrapers providing a calming view amongst the hustle and bustle below.

Chilling, kicking back and watching a couple of movies sounded like the move. I was exhausted from the hectic morning with all the additional traveling. Keenan had to be up early for work the next morning as well so we both slept in. Keenan awakens me with a kiss the next morning. He tells me he's heading out for work and his dad would be coming by. With unwelcoming morning breath, I tell him okay as I roll over and throw the comforter over my head to go back to sleep. I hear him chuckle as I sink back into REM sleep.

When I awake I enter his bathroom to shower and notice the colognes and other toiletries aligned on his bathroom counter. I pick them up one-by-one indulging in the scent of each container. After divulging in various scents, I turn the shower on then proceed to lay out my toiletries for my typical morning routine on his marble countertops. I let the glass doors steam up around me as I thought about my self-discipline or lack thereof. I give myself a pep-talk "Alright, Kendall. Let's see how much will-power you have. No sex, okay? Don't give in girl." But I had already lost half the battle agreeing to come in the first place. I knew what was up.

After a shower, I hear an entry beep and make my way back into the bedroom. I lock the bedroom door to finish getting dressed. I assume it is Keenan's father stopping by. I throw on some jeans and an off-the-shoulder sweater. I walk upstairs to the common area to meet Keenan's father. He introduces himself as pops and follows up with "You must be Kendall." I answer with a "Yes sir, how are you?" He answers in a casual yet polite demeanor. He informs me of all the errands he has to run and offers for me to join him. After accepting the invitation, he takes me around NY showing me different local areas, land marks, and scenery while knocking off items on his to-do list. We stopped for hotdogs, at a local favorite, and sat down and just discussed life and our stance on certain topics. He gave me a little background of him and Keenan and showed me the church he attends as he now lives in NY as well. We clicked. I enjoyed him explaining his beliefs and appreciated his candor speech all while he played some of his favorite tunes. His view of family reminded me of mine and we shared common views making him relatable. We were laughing and having a good ol' time. One of the errands consisted of grocery shopping so I helped him put the groceries away once we returned back to Keenan's spot. He cut on the TV in the living room and a reality TV show appeared. He inquired "You don't watch this stuff do you?" I answer, "I use to in college but is not my thing anymore. It's too wild." He laughs while saying "my girl!" He tosses the remote to me while saying "here, find something to watch." He goes to the kitchen to start cooking. I flip through a few channels before landing on a Nas documentary. We chat about Nas which naturally leads to other conversation and before long we both have fallen asleep in the living room with full stomachs.

It is now evening and I awake to Keenan standing over me smiling, he whispers, "I see you've met my dad." I smile back and softly say, "Yeah, he's a cool dude and he cooked for me."

"And you ate it?!" Keenan asks with concern.

"Yeah?! Was I not supposed to? It tastes fine to me..?" I inquire.

"Man, you have to watch him. Some of the stuff he uses be suspect," he replies with laughter.

I shrug, well too late for that now. Thanks for the heads up.

"I'm 'bout to shower but I brought you some food if you're still hungry." He says as he makes his way to his room.

I sit on the couch flipping through channels before I decide to head into the kitchen, leaving Keenan's dad snoring on the couch. I'm not hungry but the aroma is enticing. I grab a fork and saucer just to test out the entrée. The dish was really good but I decided against stuffing myself. While washing the dishes,

Keenan fresh from a shower comes behind me and wraps his arms around me, I think to myself "I can get use to this, these nice warm embraces." He starts to fix his plate and simultaneously asks "You're not going to eat?" I shake my head no but inform him I tried it and the food was good. After thanking him for the consideration I head off to take a shower, myself.

Upon exiting the shower sporting nothing but a towel, I'm greeted by Keenan lying on the bed. I sit on the bed applying lotion to my body but before I finish, Keenan sits up and starts rubbing my shoulders which entices me to lay down for a backrub. The massage is so soothing and relaxing, so I return the favor. We talk for a few hours about the most random things until we both fall asleep. I awaken to Keenan dressing quietly. He recognizes I'm awake and comes over to kiss me and said he will have to go to work, but he would be back soon. I'm a little upset as I thought I would be able to roll over and cuddle but that was not going to be the case. He only has the bathroom light on as he fidgets in one of his dresser drawers. I motion for him to come over and he does. I draw him in and place his hand below. We start kissing intimately. He groans, "You're going to have me late for work." I reply, "Just a quickie."

Turns out the pep talk I gave myself earlier was a fail but I have learn to count the small victories. Some progress was evident in me deciding against cooking for Keenan which crossed my mind while I was out running errands with his dad. As the old saying goes, "why buy the cow when you can get the milk for free?"

Later on after he was officially done with work we opted to eat at home to watch a movie. We stayed up talking about life and my future plans. It led to him asking if I would move to New York City. I share my hesitation as it would pull me from family. He assures me it would be a smooth transition. I tell him I have plans for my career which is just beginning, therefore, it needs my utmost attention. He states he understands but asks again for safekeeping. While his persistence makes me smile I change the topic.

The following morning, Keenan takes me to the airport but, once there, I realize I don't have my wallet. I go into instant panic mode because I never leave anything of importance. I try to recall the last time I had my wallet when it suddenly dawns on me that I left it under pops' passenger seat. Keenan's dad was nice enough to stop what he was doing to bring me my wallet which was a blessing in disguise because I was able to say my goodbyes to him in person. I thank them both for such a great visit after a couple of hugs and one kiss. I walk into the terminal, rolling my luggage behind me, feeling ditzy for leaving my wallet yet relieved that I didn't miss my flight. I board the plane and relax in the seat ready to reminisce the past few days. Deep down I was flying back feeling subpar and unfulfilled.

Chapter 19:
Nice For What

"HAPPY NEW YEAR!"

Everyone shouts as the clock strikes midnight. We toast glasses and hug one another. I can't resist the urge to repeatedly glance at my phone as the New Years' text notifications roll in. I anticipate one in particular. This specific person does not make the list of texts. I don't know why I expect such from him. I blow it off and decide not to let it ruin my night.

I'm out and about with Zoe, Sierra, and Bianca; we are currently at a house party cheering on some helpless soul who is chugging beer from some carved ice sculpture meant to mess people up expeditiously. After making various stops, we end up at a get together with a diverse crowd. I'm pretty intoxicated but not throw-up-able level; yet everything is funny. As the night winds down we hear one of our former teammates yell: "YALL DON'T

UNDERSTAND THE DYNAMICS OF LIFE!" He was drunk but he was right.

We return to the apartment at 3:47 in the morning and I have yet to receive a text or call from the person I wanted to hear from the most, Deshawn. I decided to swallow my pride and shoot him a Happy New Year text. I wait patiently with no reply. In frustration I throw the covers over my head and fall asleep.

The next morning I wake up to an unresponded text. I'm disappointed but more so at myself. Why do I continue to do this to myself? Why am I stuck on him? He's handsome but not THAT dang handsome. My conscience yells at me "Girl, get a grip!" She's right! I delete the text thread between he and I and choose to wish a Happy New Year to everyone that I was too incoherent, or actually lazy and self-absorbed, to respond to prior. I proceed to the living room and sink into the warmth of the couch. I grab the remote and cut the TV on to catch some bowl games, thinking it'll help me take my mind off the nonsense. LSU and Miami are playing. I toss the remote on the coffee table when my phone lights up.

"Just passing through your city, thought about you." reads the text from Deshawn. I recall he never said Happy New Year to me. I'm flattered but I come back to reality, to the fact that he doesn't want me perse, just what's between my legs. I reply with a basic "aww...that's sweet." He does not respond back.

A month pass and I receive a text the day after Valentine's Day. At first, it didn't register to me that it was the day after Valentine's Day, aka "National Side-Chick Day." Needless to say the convo went absolutely nowhere. I informed him that I was now celibate in which he told me he respected my decision. He further asks how I was doing, which caused me to believe he had a genuine interest in me and not just my body. I went into great detail about what I was now doing and how I was working on further advancing my career but, yet again, no response. That was the last straw. I took his nonresponse as if he did not give a single care but just asking out of politeness. I'd rather him not to have asked if he didn't truly mean it. Wasting my time. *sips tea*

The gag is, I wasted my own time.

Since I'm having a fresh start I get tested again, it has been a while. I have used protection with everyone, for the most part, but I'm paranoid. I never had a STD before. I decide to get tested at a clinic instead of my PCP due to the anonymity. A few days passed, that felt like weeks, no call is good news. I'm still paranoid, I need to hear the words so I call the number on the card provided to me during the testing. I give them the seven-digit code that links to my results. The other person on the end on the phone states: "You are negative for Chlamydia. You are negative for Gonorrhea. You are negative for Syphilis. You are negative for Genital Herpes. And you are negative for HIV." I let out a huge sigh of relief for a clean bill of health. "Why do I put myself through unnecessary stress; I can't keep this up," I thought to myself.

Chapter 20:
Feel No Ways

Liyah, Amber and I decided to take a girl's trip to Paris. Perfect timing as I was needing a break from my job and the men I was involved with. I figured a girl's trip would do the trick. The three of us flew from different airports but timed our flights to meet at Charles de Gaulle around the same time. Once we all landed and located one another it was on. We were so excited and happy to see each other. We finesse our way to our shuttle with broken French, arriving at our destination safely.

The hotel is beautiful, constructed with magnificent architecture. The sculptures, floral arrangements and décor are exquisite amongst the many amenities and activities the resort have to offer. We are ready to dive in and plan out our week to get the most out of our vacation. We are taken on a tour of the fancy hotel accompanied by light refreshments and hors d'orderves. After settling into our suite we decide to grab a bite to eat at one of the restaurants at the establishment. The food is fresh, authentic and tasty and our wine glasses were never empty. After catching up on each other's lives we decide to go back and call it a night as everyone is tired from traveling. I unpack my things and shower; assembling by outfits – planned well in advance – throughout the stay of our trip. Once I have all my items situated I climb in the bed and drift to sleep.

The next morning we decide to tackle our list of the main tourist attractions and highly recommended local eateries. While conversing with the locals I picked up that one spot was being recommended above the rest. It was a night club for young adults. We could truly embrace the culture genuinely and of course meet cute guys. My friends and I plan to have a night on the town. Later that evening, we decide to make a stop at the three highest recommended places, saving the number one spot, per the locals, for last.

Our first stop is a hookah lounge that plays all the throwbacks from the 90s. It has a pretty chill vibe but we're ready to dance so we cut our stay short and move on to location number two on our list. This place is promising as the music is good and the bar is top notch in appearance and service. It is a nice mix of tourists and locals so the DJ tailors the music as such. Dancing the night away, as admirers order us drinks while simultaneously providing nods and winks from afar. The club starts to wind down. One guy approaches me and suggests we go to the local favorite. I smile at the convenience of it all. I turn to my friends to see if they are still down. But they reply "tomorrow" ..."I'm tired." I don't want to go solo with a complete stranger so I ride back with my friends to the resort which was not far. The hotel so graciously provides transportation to and from.

The same gentleman from before approached me once again. Through his thick French accent he asks if I was calling it a night but offers his protection and guaranteed safety if I still want to go out. His comforting charm leads me to trust this complete stranger. I inform my friends that I'll be back as I decided to take him up on his offer. They try to talk me out of this potential *Taken* situation but I assure them I would stay in constant communication with them.

This stranger, named Jaivin, promises that I'm in good hands as he extends his arm for me to latch on to. This last club is only a short walk. We cut through back alleys and stroll through a common marketplace, down a street where we could hear the echo through the streets. The journey to the location had me nervous due to the catcalling and whistling but Jaivin would tell me to stay close to him. I felt shielded with him. Once there, the place is live and packed. Everyone is dancing and the lighting is just right. Jaivin is a great dancer as he leads me through various dances. I'm impressed. His smile draws me in and I'm simultaneously falling for Jaivin and his charm. He brings me a beverage and introduces me to some local friends. This was their hangout spot.

As the night winds down, there is a light rain that starts to fall. One of the gentlemen I dance with asks what he needs to do to receive a kiss from me. He was an innocent admirer but was politely denied. Right on cue, Jaivin comes from behind and throws his arm around me, marking his territory. We decide to head back before the bottom drops out. Jaivin leads me back to the resort while holding my hand. Before we make it back, he leads me to a nearby park and asks me if I enjoyed the night. I tell him I had a great time as I go in to hug him but he kisses me on the cheek. I look up at him and our eyes lock. We kiss one another. My adrenaline is pumping and I'm not sure if I'm making the best decision. I'm tipsy and attracted to this athletic built French local, but I don't know him from Adam. While the rain is lightly falling on us he unbuckles my grey distressed jeans. I ask him if he has protection. He nods his head and pulls a condom from his pocket. I go with the flow and allow Jaivin to experience this foreign exotic beauty. Jaivin feels good but I feel dirty. After we finish he walks me back to the resort and hugs me goodbye.

The next morning Liyah and Amber are ready to grab breakfast; I have a stubborn hangover but I still manage to make it to breakfast. I decide not to tell them what all happened last night but I did include them in on how much fun they missed out on. I tell them we needed to go back together before we return to the States. I sell them on my experience, so they agree to come with me, next time around.

After breakfast I inform them I will be staying in as I need to lay down and recuperate from last night. I insist that they go ahead and carry out the plans we have for the day without me. After a lengthy back and forth, I finally convince them to enjoy the city while I recover. I decide to enjoy the hotel amenities after sleeping most of the afternoon away. I come across tennis courts and resolve to have a go at it. While checking out a tennis racket I notice a familiar person on one of the courts. It was Jaivin, playing with his shirt off, working up a sweat. After finishing up a match with an older gentleman he comes over and asks me if I would like to play him. I told him I was just trying it out as I've only played a few times. He informs me he's an instructor then elects to show me some pointers by coming behind and guiding my hand, demonstrating the proper way to swing. He demonstrates how it's more technique than just swatting at balls aimlessly. The lesson has a level of intimacy to it that catches me off guard. Jaivin starts speaking to me in French although I am unable to fully comprehend everything he is saying but I'm hypnotized by his foreign words. He takes my hand and leads me to the restroom and locks the door behind us. He unties my shorts and slowly lowers down my panties as I stand shocked at the event that is unfolding. He kisses my inner thigh and makes his way up…

I leave the male's restroom, embarrassed on the inside but I display a facade that I'm totally unbothered. Why do I keep doing this? I know it's wrong and I feel so bad afterwards but I'm addicted. He takes me to a nearby eatery and we discuss his family, what a typical day in Jaivin's life is like, and a few French lessons with discussions of famous musical artists. It's now dark out as I decide to go back to the resort. With perfect timing Liyah and Amber have just made it back from their day of adventure. We exchange stories of our day and decide to visit the Eiffel Tower and Louvre Museum the next day. I left the rendezvous session with Jaivin out of my day recap as I didn't need the judgment that would surely ensue; I was doing a fond job of beating myself up. Seeing how everyone is worn out we all decided to stay in for the night and watch a movie together, just the three of us.

The next couple of days were spent sightseeing and purchasing little trinkets, souvenirs, perusing books found in Shakespeare and Company and buying various artwork from a plethora of local vendors. The trip ends with one more night out at the famous location I enjoyed with Jaiven. Amber and Liyah enjoyed themselves, as did I. Jaivin was unfortunately nowhere to be found. That didn't damper our plans as we dance the night away totally ignoring the fact that we each have flights to catch in hours. The following morning we manage to make it to the airport in time. I never said bye to Jaivin he remained my little secret.

After this trip I realized I truly needed to get it together. No more straddling the fence. What started as retaliation grew into bondage, I had lost control. I messed up even initiating my retaliation as Romans 12:17 states "Do no repay anyone evil for evil. Be careful to do what is right in the eyes of everyone." Completely forgetting the fact that "Whoever digs a pit will fall into it; if someone rolls a stone, it will roll back on them" (Prov 26:27). I indeed created this monster. Realizing that fact, I started to invest my time in the church by attending services, volunteering to serve, and I even joined a dance team. I started to surround myself with other young ladies who embodied the mentality I was taking on. I took a job at a hospital as it gave me the experience I needed while I was enrolled in courses at a local university. Hanging with my old friends became difficult as I was not willing to attend night clubs and turn up. I could no longer relate so my appearances tapered off. My friendship dynamics shifted as I was embracing my new self which resulted in me losing some friends. The transition was difficult but I begin to blossom into something more beautiful, like a caterpillar to a butterfly. Growth is uncomfortable and sometimes painful but necessary, trust the process.

Chapter 21:
Torn

I am debating whether I should head back to Virginia to see Keenan. I knew I wasn't strong enough to fight my sexual urges and I told Keenan that beforehand. He expressed how he respects my decision to be celibate and wouldn't do anything I would not want to. He claimed my presence was all he wanted. I call Liyah and asks her advice on the situation. She recommends that I give him a try and if he does anything then I'll know where we stand. I agree with her suggestion as it is a logical approach and decided I would make the trip.

I take off work from the hospital for a few days and text Keenan informing him that I'll come and visit him at training camp. He replies telling me he is excited to see me and how happy he is that I decided to come. In all honesty, I'm elated to be seeing him as well but deep down I am harboring an uneasy feeling. I'm in a different headspace than last year.

I don't leave early in the morning like the previous season but instead leave at night. I'm still up and figure I can make the drive to him since I'm coming from Georgia. I leave late to ensure the "coast is clear" since they are on a curfew. It always tickles me to hear they have curfew, although we had curfew during college track meets, but these are grown men. Keenan tells me which stairwell to take, what turns to make on what hallway and so on. I feel like Lara Croft on a secret mission. I admit that the risk of getting caught sneaking in is an adrenaline rush and took me back to when I use to sneak out of my house in high school.

It is now early morning but I have arrived to Keenan's room. I pull out my phone from my back pocket to let him know I have arrived. He comes to the door greeting me with a smile and a hug. He proceeds to tell me the "door was unlocked." I reply, "Well, I didn't know." I walk in further and Ben, one of his training camp teammates, is chilling on the other queen bed. Suddenly there's a knock on the door and Keenan gets up and peers through the peephole ensuring the coast is clear, he opens the door to allow two more teammates to enter. After a brief introduction, they grab game controllers, and pull up to a hyper-focused game of *Madden*. I sit on the bed and listen to them go back and forth, throwing rude but hilarious insults at one another. One of the guys picks my team in which Keenan states, "Not those bums. That's her team, while shaking his head, You're not loyal." Buddy chuckles and takes the lead over his opponent. Keenan who is laying on the bed, I'm sitting on leans over to me and asks if I have seen the new NWA film. I shake my head, no. He offers to take me to go see it. He starts looking up times on his phone and asks me if I thought I could fit everyone into my car. I imagine these giant muscle-bound men making my vehicle look like a circus clown car. I answer with hesitation, explaining it would be a tight squeeze. He follows up with "We'll make it work." Despite my uncertainty, we agree on a evening show. His friends leave to go eat and ask if we want to join them. I express that I am not hungry at the moment so Keenan declines the invite. He tells his teammates that we would see them in a few. They all file out of the room informing us they'd see us later. As soon as everyone exited the room Keenan comes closer to me in a strong yet passionate manner. He whispers in a deep, breath-taking voice, "Man, I've missed you." He picks me up and throws me on the other bed. I'm taken aback but turned on at the same time. He manages to dial it back and stop at a kiss. I'm relieved at the gesture. "That almost happen," I thought, "But he did reel it back in, maybe he really is trying?" ESPN is on and my favorite team is the main headline for the current show. He smirks, cuts his eyes at me and changes the channel while anticipating my reaction. I decide against indulging in my pettiness and grab my laptop which displays a collage on my laptop background. He points at a specific picture, "when are you going to wear my jersey?" I smile, maybe someday. He repeats my response in confusion "some day?! What will it take for you to become a fan?" I laugh when I tell him, "A lot." He probes "like what?" As he reaches for my laptop. I move it further from him, so that he cannot touch it. He teases me for still using a laptop while everyone else is using tablets and phones. I nudge him for making fun of me. He reaches for it once again. On my computer he pulls up a special account. With an air of confidence he requests I pick out a nice pair of shoes. I tell him to make the selection and surprise me. He asks for my favorite colors and size. Feeling brazen, he informs me he ordered some he thinks I will like. "We shall see" I respond. As the conversation begins to get deep, discussing school and my plans to become a nurse practitioner. His words are encouraging and his belief in how I'm going to be great were deposits in an emotional bank I was unaware of. I was emotionally invested. We hear a knock on the door, it's time to head to the movies.

These four NFL players, all 6 feet and above, burly men all try to fit into my Altima. I'm sitting in between two of them while Keenan drives us to the theater. Although the space was tight it made for a great memory as it was a funny, yet bizarre, bonding moment. Bizarre as I felt out of place in this whole ordeal only knowing one of the four guys yet we all laughed and clicked as if this was not my first appearance. The sight of everyone climbing out of the car was probably even funnier, but we made it. The little engine that could is what came to my mind. The movie theater is just about empty but we find out that we aren't the only ones who had the bright idea to go see a movie. About seven or eight of Keenan's other teammates have arrived in a van. They convinced one of the team's drivers to take them.

I carry my icee and Raisinets, courtesy of Keenan, into the theater following Ben with Keenan closely behind me. In my mind Keenan took me out on a date. I was happy. Granted his teammates were there it still felt like a date, just a lot of third-wheelers accompanying us. During the movie I would answer Keenan's questions concerning the storyline and he would catch me singing along with the songs. At one point, he asks "Yo, how do you know so much? You're the same age as me." I laugh, "Yeah, but I'm hip and very versatile." He shakes his head and sarcastically said "sure."

After gathering together once the movie ended, one of his teammates who did not ride with us loudly broadcasts a question "Who is that?!" Keenan closes the gap between us and calmly said "that's me, bruh." I smile, still moving forward. His teammate replies, "Oh that's you? You know I'm thirsty." The short amount of time I've been at the training camp location I understand the "act now, ask questions later" mentality.

The next morning, the alarm goes off and I hop in the shower, get dressed and make my way to the practice field. I grab the extra room key and lanyard that was left behind for me. I also notice money was left on the nightstand for me. I'm taken aback. Keenan informs me via text he left gas money on the nightstand and that he will be staying a little longer to rehab. He suggests I head back after the first session as he'll be at the facility until the afternoon session. I decide to take his advice due to the unbearable heat. I grabbed lunch at a nearby restaurant. I pay for my meal and head back to the resort. Once off the elevator I take a Gatorade Frost and bottled water from the fridge located in the common area beside the elevator. These fridges were located on every floor to ensure players remained hydrated. I make my way to the room, passing by some of the players who are on hoverboards zooming up and down the hall, just cooling. I enter the room before anyone really notices me.

The panini I purchased is pretty good but I'm disappointed with my cookies, the sole reason I went. They are burnt. I decide to sit the team's next session out while they do walkthroughs. Instead I walk around the resort noticing various ongoing events, even a wedding reception outdoors in the "garden". While exploring, I receive a text from an old homie checking in on me. It had been a minute since we talked. I told him how I would like a male insight in a situationship I was in. I felt my judgment of the situation was irresponsible at worst and flawed at best. His response to me:

"Obviously you like him but if he's not going to commit to celibacy why keep him around? Unless you're going to break your vows. It's going to be an ongoing complicated process but you know this already. It's like you don't want to lose him but you don't want to break your vow either. You're going to have to choose. I understand what he's doing Kay but what are you doing? That's the puzzling part. ...You're never going to move on and see what else is out there if you keep thinking about this dude.

When a person tells the person they're sleeping with that they decided to go celibate. If that person wants to be with you then automatically it would become obvious that they would have to do the same. I shouldn't have to ask them to do it. And the vibe I'm getting from him is he still wants to f*** with you but not date you. What is he waiting for? He's trying to make you feel bad. When in reality he could just take the next step and ask to date you and go celibate. That simple. He wants to still fool around Kay. Come on *you're a smart girl. It's pretty obvious. Trust me, I've lived that life. Yall have already slept together so it's not like he'd have something to look forward to. No offense to you but let's be real here.*

...I just told you why. So he can f*** other chicks and have you when he's done because he knows Kendall is going to probably still be feeling sorry (like you do now) and accept him back. Kay think about it. You play all tough and s*** but who you fooling? You're sweet as hell, educated, and funny as s***. What guy wouldn't want to wife you when they're done f****** around and want to settle down bra. He's keeping you around and you don't see it because you're caught up in your feelings for him."

I hear him, but I'm not listening. Keenan is different. I tell him "thanks" and swipe the thread away. It's getting dark so I go back to the room anticipating Keenan's arrival but I'm now becoming hungry again. I wait at least another 30-45 minutes before I start researching food spots on my phone. I have the taste for Chinese food but there aren't any places nearby. The place considered the closest is in some strip mall in the middle of nowhere. I read a few reviews and decide to make the trip. I ended up near a small airport that hosted small private planes but there are no restaurants in sight. I'm annoyed with my GPS and now entering the "you need a snickers" phase of hunger. I try a different route and another place comes up approximately twenty minutes from my "middle of nowhere" location. I make the drive to a suspicious looking place that screams "stranger danger." I place my order to go and opt to wait in my car. After obtaining my order I book it back to the resort with my food still warm upon arrival. As soon as I wash my hands and sit down Keenan and Ben enters. He jokes about me not getting him anything to eat. I laugh but he was semi-serious. I retort with assuming he and his friends had already eaten since they were gone so long. He replies, "we did but I can eat again." I try to finish my dinner but for some reason I always become full whenever Keenan is around. He looks at me, "that's all you eating?" I nod with embarrassment and offer him the rest. He takes a bite "Aye, this hitting," furthering inquiring where I got the food from. I tell him about my voyage to get Chinese food, which peaked with ending up in a suspect area. He cautions me to be more careful as the people from that area are unpredictable.

"Aye, Ben, try this."

His roommate grabs a fork and relishes with Keenan on the stellar taste. They inhale my leftovers as I watch, judging them in my mind. What savages?

"Never trust Chinese food from the mall, or is it the airport? I can't remember, one of them isn't right," said Keenan. I shake my head and laugh. Ben flips to a movie that we all have seen. Keenan cuts the lights off. He does not give the film much attention.

We hear a knock on the door. Keenan looks at his roommate. I instantly slide off the bed onto the floor, lying between the two beds with my back against Keenan's hoping the comforter can cover me enough to not be seen, getting him in trouble. Someone comes to the door for a room check but refrains from a more thorough check. They exchange a few words and move on to the next room. We all carry on as if nothing happens. I crawl back into Keenan's bed and he places the comforter over both of us. He starts to kiss me and reels me in closer to him. I can feel every light touch of his lips from my neck to my midback. I hear Ben enter the bathroom. Keenan is no longer holding back his urges. He slides in slowly but abruptly stops, pausing momentarily as he asks "You want me to stop?" I hesitantly shake my head no as he is already inside me at this point. I'm nervous, waiting for Ben to walk out of the bathroom at any second. Keenan and I are really going at it: moans, sweat, bed knocking, bedding in a disarray and on the floor. Just exposed. Once we calm down,

Ben re-enters the room. I quickly grab a sheet when I hear the bathroom door turn. I'm embarrassed by my predicament. I go to the bathroom adorning a bedsheet. Keenan follows behind me, we shower and throw on enough clothes for Ben's sake. I tiptoe back to the bed in hopes to not further disturb him. I fall asleep in Keenan's embrace, cuddling with him. I feel safe, protected, wanted and loved in a sense.

We sleep in as the team was granted the day off. Well, I should say I slept in. Keenan woke up early to return to the facility for rehab and treatment. I okayed him using my car beforehand so he could sleep in longer. By the time he returned it was around noon. He takes me to a place on the resort, a nice little southern upscale restaurant. I order a sweet tea and a fried green tomato sandwich that is topped with Chèvre Cheese, spinach, BBQ Spiced Bacon, Shaved Red onions and black pepper mayo. All of which is served on fine china. I feel like I'm at a legitimate adult tea party. My tea even comes with a dish for the syrup to sweeten to my liken. This restaurant is exquisite. Keenan laughs at my selection of food stating "You don't want that." I reply, "I do." I eat some and then the "Keenan effect" kicks in again so I decide to take the remainder back to the room. Keenan ended up finishing it off in which he agreed it was good.

Later that night, we discuss plans for my career in details; in which he informs me that I can do all of that where he lives. Déjà vu. Ben returns about three hours later and I blush at the thought of last night. The latest Terminator is playing in the background as I tell Keenan about an incident at one of his practices yesterday. I inform him that I ran into a man who was asking how I knew him and what was my name and number. With a google search I found out that the guy was a reporter. Keenan laughs it off as if the dude was just trying to holler; but no, it was not that type of vibe at all. "I hope this doesn't come back and bite him," I thought.

But what you want to do for dinner? He asks. I'm not really in the mood to go anywhere, I respond. Okay, he tosses me a menu. What you want? I look over the rather overpriced menu and opted for a salad and pizza. He asks questionably, "Are you going to eat it?" Yes! You just have this effect on me. He replies, "Yeah, you're too grown for that" as he laughs. I give him a playful shove and he wrestles me to the bed. After tossing and wrestling for a while he tells Ben "She's stronger than some of the guys in the league and she's quick." "Of course I'm quick, I ran track." Oh shut up, he said jokingly, "You want more?" I ask. He replies, "I have almost 200 pounds on you." Yeah, and? He chuckles, "do you not recall me just balling you up?" I answer, "nah; I think you're mistaken. But just let me know when you ready to get beat again. He laughs, "Yeah, okay." Ben states, "Okay, I know what I want." Keenan replies, "Cool, call in the order and I'll pay for it." While we are awaiting room service they discuss the coaches and other players' personalities as I sit entertained. It was as if I was engaging in a behind the scene reel. Their renditions and impersonations of their teammates and staff had me laughing hysterically. While they were in the middle of their standup we hear a knock on the door and a male voice said "Room Service." Keenan opens the door and generously tips the guy. My pizza is personal and the salad was amazing, super fresh ingredients. But yet again, I get full during the salad. Keenan just looks at me and shakes his head; "my son who is 5 can eat more than that." Ughh shut it, it's your fault," in my defense it was truly uncontrollable. He laughs, "I'm just saying."

That night ended with laughs and cuddling. The next morning it was time for me to hit the road yet again. Once more, Keenan entices me to stay but I manage to escape his persuasion. If I could have stayed longer, I would have. I was happy with him. When morning hit I said my goodbyes to Keenan and Ben. Keenan walks me to my car commenting on my favorite NFL team car emblem to his disdain. I tell him it's staying. He presses me hard about devotion. I clap back with a sharp retort. "Alright, I want to end on a good note. I hope I get to see you again." I reply, "We shall see." I get in the car preparing to make the drive back but I also feel defeated. Defeated for not upholding celibacy, the money on the nightstand fiasco – even though I knew the intent – and putting myself in temptation instead of fleeing. My feelings were invested, I don't want to say goodbye to Keenan but knew I needed to. I was falling for him but I was also dealing with the strong possibility that he may not be the one for me. My homie may have been on to something. Staying in a situationship versus honoring God, talk about being torn in between two.

Chapter 22:
Where I Wanna Be

The following is text between Keenan and I

Me: You sleep

Keenan: No you sleep. He funny af.

Me: Ha! You're ready to square up over him huh?

Keenan: Lol naw we ain't gotta box about it

Me: I know, I was jk'n

Keenan: We can square up about your boyfriend tho

Me: What bf? *Confused emoji*

Keenan: Buddy you just took a trip with

Me: That's not my bf. We discussed this

Keenan: Well whatever he is to you

Me: A friend. I'm at church so I can't lie lol. I wouldn't lie anyways

Keenan: You call me "a friend" too.

Me: You're more than a friend... we did not have sex. I'm not interested in him like that. But... You've slept/sleep with people so it shouldn't make a difference.

Keenan: I never said you did. You ain't gotta have sex with somebody for them to be more than just "a friend." And you don't know what I do. I was just asking.

Me: This is true, but I'm telling you he's not. You right, but you told me you have before, so I went to be retested. Okay. Anymore questions?

Keenan: No ma'am. Sorry.

Me: Whelp. I have one. Why didn't you ask "this" sooner? You were conversating with me during that trip

Keenan: Cause it's technically not my business

Me: Oh. That was the deciding factor lol

Keenan: But I just thought it wouldn't hurt to ask

Me: Would it have made a difference?

Keenan: No

Me: Figured that much

Keenan: What you mean?

Me: I figured it wouldn't make a difference either way

Keenan: Why you say that tho?

Me: Cause I don't hear from you for months

Keenan: We've talked about this before. You don't want me.
Only way for me to get over you is not talking to you.

Me: I never said I don't want you, never

Keenan: That's just how it seemed

Me: How?

Keenan: We talked about this Kendall!

Me: We have. Idk how it came off as that tho.

TWO WEEKS LATER

Keenan: Good morning Kendy!

Me: Good morning Key!

K: You're beautiful!! I miss you

Me: Thanks handsome. I miss you too!

FATHER'S DAY

Me: Happy Father's Day!!

K: Thank you!!

ONE WEEK LATER

K: *kiss emoji*

Me: Dang, Professor X, I was just thinking about you.

K: Noooo you wasn't

Me: Yes, I was. Why was that no so drawn out tho?

K: Lol cause you lying

Me: I'm not, I really was thinking about you earlier. Why would I lie?

K: What about me were you thinking about?

Me: Just how you were. What you were doing? How's life treating you. The usual…

K: Awww. Obviously I was thinking about you too

Me: I guess

K: I was

K: And I do

Me: You told me you were tired of our "cycle" so I stopped hitting you up.

Context: Back story on our "cycle"… Him requesting we get together with promises we won't have sex then we end up having sex and me feeling bad. I kept saying one thing and doing another. The cycle.

K: That's what I did

Me: Difference between me and you tho is you said the above so…

K: I stopped hitting you up to stop the "cycle."

Me: Well…now what?

K: I was telling you I was thinking about you and I miss you

Me: I'm saying the feeling is mutual; we both know that

K: Can I see you?

Me: As in…?

K: In person

Me: I mean, I still feel the same way tho…

K: Are you willing to come?

Me: To?

K: Here

Me: Yeah, IF we're on the same page

K: I have two different places. So you can stay at one and I can stay the other.

Me: That's what it takes? If I came it would be to be around you not divided so-to-speak

K: I'm great with being around you. I'm doing that for your comfort

Me: Way to think ahead lol

K: Trying

Me: I respect it

NEXT DAY

K: Good morning

Me: Good morning

K: We didn't come up with nothing

Me: I know. Okay, let's try it

K: Okay great. When do you want to come?

Me: You have a time frame in mind?

K: When are you off?

Me: End of the month. I'll have to move some things around anyways so I'm asking for how long?

K: Oooh d***. Just a couple of days

K: like ASAP

Me: Umm… Potentially 2-6th or 3-6th

K: 3-6th would actually be perfect

Me: Okay, that will work

K: I got you

I'm picked up at the airport with *Drip Too Hard* flowing through the car speakers. While riding with Keenan to a gated community, he requests that we walk around in robes. The security guard tips his hat as Keenan drives through the opening bronze entrance gates. The mansions resemble castles. I admire the landscaping and architect work of the homes. We pull up to Keenan's home and the entrance double doors make him appear small which is saying a lot in reference to this 6'5 300-pound man. He opens the door for me as I roll one of my luggage bags behind me. I come to the realization that I love his new home and I'm only standing in the foyer. He places my other bags by the staircase while asking if I would like to see the house. "Of course I would like a tour!" We take a tour of the mansion wth multiple rooms, theater, kitchen, garden terrace, jacuzzi, and more. After the tour I tell him how happy I am for him and that I really like his new home. He then informs me that he is having a pool table delivered and assembled in a few. I am entrusted with the responsibility of signing off for it. Keenan has to leave to go to work. I sink into the pleasant, comfy, yet sophisticated, cream-colored U-sectional. I prop my feet up, wrapped in cozy socks, on the ottoman as I prepare to indulge in my current read, *Gentlewoman*. The TV plays softly in the background but I tune it out as I continue to read. That wasn't the only thing I tuned out. I receive a call from Keenan, "Hey K, you sleep?" I answer, "No, why you ask?"

He replies, "The guys said they've been outside ringing the doorbell and no one has answered."

I hurry to the door and see a truck parked out front. I quickly open the door and motion the guys to come in. I tell Keenan "they're in now" as I chuckle. He thanks me and tells me he'll be home shortly. I apologize to the guys but they're really professional and friendly about the whole ordeal. I go back to reading as they go back and forth retrieving tools and materials from the boxed white truck parked outside. Keenan walks in as they ask which way he would like the pool table facing. He looks to me for my opinion, but I tell him he should let the crew decide. They make a suggestion and Keenan rolls with it. Once fully assembled Keenan tips the guys as they wrap up convos and make their way to the front door. All the while, I'm back on the couch with my book. He plops down beside me "What are you reading?" I show him the title, sharing how good it is. He utters a doubtful "Mmhmm." I laugh at his skepticism, then proceed to ask how his day was as I close my book. He goes, "I'm tired, I thought your flight was later but it all worked out and you were able to let those guys in for me; thank you." No problem, I chime. He pulls me closer to him as he surfs the channels until he lands on the movie 300. "Oh yea, my movie! You ever seen this?" he asks. "Of course," I reply, "who hasn't?" I say sarcastically. "Man this is a good movie" he blurts with excitement lining his voice. I laugh at his strong reppage - possibly just created a new word but let's roll with it- and child-like attention to the movie. While men in chariots are rolling across the screen I rest back on Keenan's chest as the daylight slowly fades away. We both fall asleep with the TV watching us but we awake with growling stomachs. "Do you like tacos? He asks and without missing a beat he continues "I know this fire taco spot!"

"Sure, let's go check it out," I reply.

"Alright, let's go" as he gets up from the couch.

We climb into the truck with all tinted windows. About 30 minutes later we pull up to a little hole in the wall, greeted with menus and warm smiles. Once seated, I notice all the team paraphernalia throughout the restaurant. It is a pretty cool site to see. I wonder if Guy Fieri has ever stopped by. This looks to be a local favorite. After going back and forth on what I want while also trying to hear Keenan and the waiter's suggestions; I finally make a decision. The appetizer is brought out, which I consume more of than Keenan. The sangria is tasty but the fish tacos are my favorite. After enjoying dinner and sharing a few laughs Keenan pays the bill, tip and we head out. To my surprise, he drives us back to his condo. Once parked, he asks if I'll come inside as he had to grab a few things.

I help Keenan carry some items to the truck and he cuts on some old school music as he jokes "You don't know nothing about this." I playfully, with a boy-bye attitude, reply "psshh… this is the Temptations, *Papa was a Rolling Stone*." The drums come through and the slow insertion of the smooth trumpet, saxophone and other instruments then the oh so familiar intro words roll in. Keenan is impressed, but will not be done up by throwing on another record. *"When a man loves a woman."*

Well, I mean the first line is the title I reply. He goes, "True, last one…" as the intro of another classic flows through the speakers.

With confidence, *"Stand by Me"*. "Yeah, you might know a little something, something" he said while smiling. We continue to listen and sing old school songs as we drive through the New York City night heading back to his house.

120

The next morning I awaken to breakfast. He didn't cook it himself for he had yet been grocery shopping. I sit at the kitchen bar as he goes through the pile of mail that he has neglected for quite some time. I guess the pile was not of importance as he tosses them to the side and grabs bottled water. He heads to a guest bathroom as I decide to tidy up the kitchen before I head to the master's bathroom to shower. While I was showering in his bathroom he was peeling the paint off the walls of another bathroom. I come out dressed in jean shorts, a coral peach high-lo tank top and brown sandals with a messy bun. He comments on how short my shorts are.

"Yeah," I respond sarcastically, "They're shorts…"

We pull up to a building in which I have the honor of helping him pick out a rug for the living room. I enjoy home décor so I was really pleased with the home store trip and exploring each other's taste in décor. After making a selection, the truck is loaded up and we grab some food to take back to the house but not before a Target run. I need to purchase some coconut oil #NaturalHairProbs. After various errands and last minute stops we finally make it back to the house, initially greeted by the friendly "community guard." I carry in the food along with our purchases as he totes the aerial rug. Somewhere between throwing decorative pillows at one another to play fighting we managed to wrestle each other out of our clothes. I couldn't help but notice the uncovered window panels by the front entrance as the thought of a peeping Tom spying on us with my goodies out on the kitchen countertops, bar, new couch, cream ottoman and elsewhere. We finally collapse together on the stairs as I'm straddling, I asks if he pulled out in time. He believes he did but is not 100% sure. I let him know I would be more at peace if I took a Plan B. He doesn't argue but hands me the keys to the truck and a $100 bill. I dress after taking a quick bird bath and hop in the truck and wave bye to the security man. I type "drug store" in GPS and continue on the closest route to me. I notice the sunset behind a beautiful cathedral as I make my way to the nearest drug store. It was such a gorgeous sight, a museum-worthy painted canvas. I pull up to the drugstore, make my purchase and scan the drugstore card on the key ring. As I head to the truck it dawns on me the keys are not mine; I just scanned someone's card out of habit.

Upon arrival back to Keenan's home I tell him of my card scanning mishap in which he tells me, "It's okay, it's my teammates."

"I know that! That's why I feel bad. What if his wife notice the Plan B on his recent purchases?!"

Keenan states, "She's not worried. It's not a problem. Relax." I take his advice and quit worrying about it as he knows the couple better than I.

We chop it up over dinner but the guilt is starting to settle in strong for me regarding our sexual encounter that occurred. I say nothing and try to carry on as normal. Keenan sits on the sectional and commands the TV to display an underground cypher. He asked me if I've seen this particular group's videos. I shake my head no as he motions me to come his way, requesting me to leave the kitchen island to accompany him on the couch. Every other line he looks at me and say "ooh…did you catch that? Fire!"

I laugh, "You really like this, huh?"

"Yeah, they're so good. You don't like it?"

"Nah, it's straight but you are truly geeked."

"Because they are geniuses, watch, you'll catch something they said later on."

"Oh whatever, I get it, I understand metaphors, similes, underlying meanings, all that"

"Right. K"

"I do," attempting to reassert myself but it may have just fallen on deaf ears.

By the time we get ready for bed, Keenan is out for the count. I tried to wake him up to discuss how I felt about having sex earlier but he was not interested in any conversation, I only get mumbles that I cannot make out. I give up on trying to express my feelings and make sure all my items are packed for my flight in the morning. I question myself, why did I wait so late to initiate this conversation that is so important to me? If I'm being real with myself, it took me that long to muster up the courage to say how I truly felt. I also admit that I am fearful as I did not want to face the aftermath of said conversation.

The next morning, very few words are exchanged. I feel the tension. He does too. It is possible he is bothered that I attempted to cut into his sleep. I am not entirely sure, but it was important to me and I was ready to talk it out at that moment. I had the courage to finally voice how I felt last night, but I settled for being slept on, literally. I wound up going to sleep that night upset and feeling ignored. We headed to the airport with me feeling as if I let myself down yet again, because I did. I can't keep doing this. The definition of insanity is doing the same thing over and over and expecting different results. I had to make a decision what I wanted more.

Chapter 23:
The Break Up Song

A couple of weeks pass by and I haven't mustered the courage to end this situationship despite feeling bamboozled and used. His birthday is coming up so I decide to send a gift with a 4-page letter but this 4-page letter has a twist. The box, which I deemed "the breakup box" contained the following:

- Birthday card (with instructions for him to read the letter last)
- Love Jones DVD (I found out he had never seen it and was shocked)
- Memorabilia of his favorite movie
- His favorite candy
- Homemade treats
- Bottle of wine (that I always wanted him to try, my favorite)

- Mini balloons (in the colors of his team)
- Pictures of us strategically placed around the decorated inner flaps of the box
- And the 4-page letter containing all the things I did not want to say but needed to say (with a burned CD with hand-selected tracks by yours truly, a few songs being: *Almost* by Tamia, *Next To You* by Ciara, *Hold On* by Xscape, *Try Sleeping With A Broken Heart* by Alicia Keys)

A week or so before his birthday I asked for his address which he provided without hesitation via text. That made my decision even harder to "end it' as that was an act of trust to me. I'm not from that area -or state even- and my sense of direction is not google maps efficient so that was the vulnerability that warmed my heart.

After gathering all the items and purchasing a sturdy cardboard box I start decorating the inside of the box with craft paper, pictures of us in various settings throughout the time we have known each other (which is roughly 2.5 years at this point). I organize the pics in a timeline fashion capturing different moments of our time together. I enjoy putting the box together until it was time to add the letter, this would make all the difference. I went back and forth, talked to Liyah who read it and told me it was well-written stating "if anything he'll understand where you're coming from." I'm so cheesy, I even created a playlist titled "If Only" and burned it to a CD to accompany the letter as he read it. Honestly, he probably tossed the CD and never played it. Who knows…but the four page letter read as follow:

Keenan,

    Feel free to play the CD while you're reading this Where do I start? Heck! How do I start? I hope you enjoyed your birthday! My last visit with you confirmed what I've been trying to ignore… I feel as if you know where this is headed BUT WAIT! Don't ball this up and throw it away just yet, hear me out please.

False Start: A Record of Experiences

I remember when we first met in Pensacola, I'll never forget that trip because I met you. You're such a chill, laid-back individual with a good heart. I like how you keep true to yourself, you haven't let money change you. You seem like an awesome dad (family-oriented), a leader, self-sufficient, you're athletic (an all-around athlete to let you tell it lol), honest, have a sense of humor, you make me laugh & even laugh at my corniness, and you make me smile. Ha! You're like a big cuddly bear lol hahahaha. All qualities I want in a man which is why I stuck around longer than I should have. I told you from the jump I didn't want to be in a situationship...guess what tho...this is a SITUATIONSHIP! I'm not one to play house. I'm not one to force something either. With that said, I believe we want two different things. I respect your desires and your stance on what you currently want as far as the relationship goes. But I don't feel that respect is reciprocated, here's why:

You know I'm practicing celibacy hence why I kept my distance from you cause CLEARLY being around each other leads to sex. You told me numerous times you respect my decision, however; actions speak louder than words. I can't figure out why the cycle kept continuing. Better yet, I can't figure out why I kept allowing it. Nah, I'm lying, I trusted you that's why. With that said, I felt like you abused that trust. Maybe you think/thought I was playing hard to get. I promise you that's not the case. I took a vow and I'm honoring God by saving myself until marriage. So that sexual encounter will be the last time I have sex until marriage. Man, listen, I started my celibacy over at least 3 times (training camp, All Star Weekend, and this). This pattern has to end. I'm holding myself back from reaching my full potential. Yes, you read correctly, I feel as this sexcapade is blocking my blessings, it's distorting my view i.e. I don't see things for what they are between us.

I don't want you to be offended by this nor feel attacked. I'm trying to be completely honest and display my feelings and stance on this entire situation. I'm generally not one to share my feelings easily; I try to remain optimistic at all times and therefore not dwell on issues which in turn, I may not give proper attention to issues that may deserve a more in-depth review. But this particular issue has been bothering me for THE longest but I kept trying to appease everyone in this equation which is not feasible right now.

What's REALLY wild, one of my homeboys read me like a book AND I still went to see you... ain't that some ish?! I don't know if you're familiar with soul ties but that joint is REAL. I can attest to it myself, I know I have a soul tie with you without a doubt. They're created with sex, amongst other things, but that's a topic for another time. Feel free to research it in your free time (but be mindful of what you read, guard your heart with all diligence). Anywho, at your last training camp this particular friend told me without knowing who you were or anything of the sort. I gave him an overview, minus specifics and details. His POV and that conversation was eye-opening for me.

HE READ ME LIKE A BOOK! That was my wakeup call right there but against better judgment AGAIN I went to see you and broke my vow, again. The thing about breaking the vow is that it is a HUGE deal to me, I always feel like crap afterward. Although it feels good at that present moment, it's not worth the feeling of failure and heartache that ensues afterward. The paranoia I experience going to get tested; yes, I got tested again, today btw. The filth that consumes me, no amount of showers can wash away. I'm not saying that God punishes me afterward but something always happens: last time I had a relative become sick and was in ICU for months, the medical staff was discussing power of attorney, and counting them out. I prayed, along with my family, around the clock. I set by their bedside and cried my heart out and told them stories from the past to how my day went that day. I refused to count them out, my faith is strong. I also appreciate your prayers for them during that trying time. Then after this recent sexual encounter I lost two family members this past week and you got injured, again. Again, I'm not saying this is God punishing me, or us for that matter, but I failed, I gave into temptation. My belief is this: If you give in to temptation you expose yourself to the devil's attacks; you're not as equipped and protected as you would have been had you not given into temptation. I keep failing to deal with you lol. Everyone's temptations are different, some battle with alcohol, some battle with drugs, and other sexual temptations...the list goes on. I'm in no position to judge others, I know exactly what my issue is and I'm trying to do my best with dealing with it. I can't please myself, you, and God at the same time unless we are on one accord. If I please you, right now, I'm essentially choosing you over God, and I'm not one for idolatry.

However, this causes me to question your respect for me and believe in God after we have sex. A man of God is a leader and leads you in the right direction. I question your respect for me because if you truly respect me you would respect my decision and help me uphold my decision, not be my downfall. You claim you respect my decision but yet it's the same outcome every time. What am I to believe? I understand you're not celibate. In no way am I judging you for not being celibate nor am I trying to force celibacy on you. It's something you have to decide on your own, something that is placed on your heart by God. So no, I don't expect you to see my reasoning for my decision or to even understand it but I do expect you to respect it.

Please do not think this is about me wanting marriage from you. Although my end goal concerning relationships is a successful marriage with whomever God has for me, one day. As of now, I'm still not ready for marriage. One step at a time. But this situationship that I'm currently in does not lead to marriage, and I'm sure of that. I'm working on becoming a lady that my future spouse will be proud to have, not just arm candy, but instead: a woman of God, a loving and nurturing mother, a force to be reckoned with, the type of lady that demands everyone's attention by her mere presence yet humble with a demeanor that evokes: stimulating intellectual convo, deep sensual emotions and respect.

"The price for sex is marriage...the price for a relationship is a commitment – It's hard to ask a man to pay for either when you're giving both for free." – Ethan O. Bereola II

Touché. OMG... Let me tell you how pissed I was when I came across that PINK label on your bedroom floor. What made me really mad was the fact that I, Kendall, put myself in that situation. An uncompromising position. I couldn't say anything about it because we weren't and aren't together. So there I was, having to sit there with the "I eat butt face." I brought it up in a joking manner but I was livid and was lowkey hurt. Again, with the expectations. I wouldn't invite you over and have some dude draws on the floor, although that has happened in my past, but I digress.

Playing house. That is what's happening here. I'm not a part-time thrill. I'm more than a weekend rendezvous. This is toxic, Keenan, and I cannot do this anymore. It's taking a toll on me and compromising my spiritual, physical, mental, and emotional health. This is putting me in a place I do not deserve nor want to be. What good is coming from this? It's going nowhere, we're like hamsters on a running wheel; horrible comparison but you get the point I'm attempting to make. I always feel dirty or used afterward. Ohhh –Emmm-Geee for example, when I went to visit you at training camp last year, I woke up with the money you left on the nightstand. My pride was like "leave it!" but being the frugal person I am my self said "Girl, that's gas money. Get over yourself." Then the last visit, you went to sleep on me...yeah, I felt used. "Like dang, we can't have some deep convo now? He listened to me talk his head off the last visit. But then again, that's been declining too...MESSAGE! Girl, getcho life!" AND last but not least, you made a snap with your baby mama. Yeah, yeah you told me she would be at the wedding and whatnot but I still felt uneasy. Reason being, males rarely post females on social media. It may sound petty but put yourself in my shoes that's suspect and appears shady, "red flag." I was cool with not being on your social media and whatnot; we're not dating, I get it. Heck, I'll probably delete all mine once I start dating, ha! But back to the subject matter at hand, that leads me to believe there's something more going on. I could be wrong, but either way, I'm falling back. I say baby mama, again I could be wrong, but your son look like homegirl in the IG story soo...it is what it is.

"Your Promise to God: I don't have time for people who keep me down. I will only invest myself in relationships that bring me closer to you." – T.D. Jakes (Promises from God for Single Women)

There's a message here. I'm not saying you're keeping me down. I'm keeping myself down. I know what I need to do and what I should have been done. Now, I'm in too deep so-to-speak. Another point, I'm not saying that you're not the guy for me... But what's meant to be will be. If you are that lucky guy lol, we both need to work on ourselves & straighten some things out before we become one.

"You teach people how to treat you by what you allow, what you stop, and what you reinforce." – Tony A. Gaskins Jr. (Single Is Not A Curse)

Facts only! I allowed it to happen, every single time! It wasn't rape, I went along with the flow. In the back of my mind I wanted it. But what I really wanted, more than sex, was for you to not tempt me, for us to go out the house, do anything to keep our minds off of sex. I get it, you're not really in the position to walk around town freely without being spotted but dang, I would have been fine with a stroll in a desolate park or something of the sort lol, but really. It would have led me to believe you were really trying, that you had a game plan. My best-friend even suggested: why don't you suggest going to bible study? I thought that was an awesome idea but I never asked out of fear of rejection, out of receiving the wrong response from you because that would have sealed the deal for me if it wasn't an answer I was anticipating, seeking, so dearly wanting. So I can't play the blame game because the fault is shared. But I'm getting it together now; I refuse to keep repeating this vicious, hurtful cycle. What good has come from this? I know for a fact that better is in store for us, regardless if we end up together or not. You know... The definition of insanity is doing the same thing over and over again and expecting different results. Smh. Something gotta give.

However, I would be doing a disservice if I did not include the good with the bad. I truly enjoyed the time we spent together, I will forever cherish those moments. They were so enjoyable they made me believe that you could be the one. I painted a false image and had expectations for us which is why I had such a hard time telling you no and essentially letting you go. Don't get me wrong, I know it will be difficult at first, but time heals right? Nah, Jesus heals, I ain't got no worries lol. On a serious note, I know it will be a challenge. You will continue to cross my mind, I'll have that itch to send you a message, or scroll through your IG. But it is best for both of us, we have different expectations. For the right man to come into my life I have to make room for him. I can't expect anything of him that I do not have in order myself and that includes, but not limited to, our situationship.

But anywho, I wish you the best in all your future endeavors; I know you will continue to soar, you're a hard worker and dedicated. Although we may never speak, you will continue to remain in my prayers K.

Forever grateful & always with love,

Kendall

"Celibacy is the heart and soul of the Wait because control over this area of instant gratification empowers you to have control over so many other areas in your life – the same ones that may have led to a repetitive pattern of heartbreak, loneliness, wasted money, and wasted time." – DeVon Franklin

After adding the letter, the Break Up Box (BUB) was fully assembled; I summon enough courage to take the box to the nearest post office and ensured it would arrive on/before his birthday. I never told Keenan why I needed his address but he would soon find out.

Two days later I text Liyah with the following message: "Idk if he opened it. He just sent a pic of the package." I wish I had the fortitude to have this conversation in person with him but I thought I would just falter as before. This was me ensuring I no longer did the same thing over and over, breaking the insanity routine. I would recommend this conversation be had in person if you know you will not jeopardize your stance.

Shortly afterward I receive a text from Keenan that reads:

"Awwwwwwww (yes, it was 8 w's, I counted) Kendall you d*** near made me cry (tear face sad emoji)! I swear this was the sweetest ever! Thank you sooo much I really appreciate it (heart kiss emoji)" I grow even more nervous as I know he couldn't have read the letter yet. I know he didn't; I instructed him not to in the card but to read it last. It's now getting to the point I just want to cut my phone off to not face the reaction that is to come next. I'm at work having a difficult time focusing because I know I just "broke up" with someone on their birthday via snail mail. I take a deep breath as various scenarios play out in my mind; before I can get my nerves fully under control my phone lights up. "Here we go," I thought to myself. I glance at the preview of the message and my stomach knots up. I open the message and without reading I respond "Okay, I'm at work. So I'm choosing not to read your response right now just in case you cause me to get in the feels."

No response.

I get home, shower and finally decide to face the reality of the situation. I open the message that reads:

"I just read your letter and of course I feel like s***. It hurts me that you think I don't respect you and that you make it seem like I force the issue. Since your celibacy I've seen you with God honest intentions. I really try my hardest not to go there with you. And I've failed more than once. I completely apologize about everything I've put you there. I'm not interested in what your "friend" had to say. He can speak on situations and experience but if he don't know me personally and the way I handle my life I would rather not take his opinion. But anyway I respect you with the utmost. I'm truly sorry it's gotten this bad. I don't want to be a burden or stop your growth. I wish you all the best Kendall Smith in everything you do in life. Much success and blessings *Praise hands emoji*""

Of course I'm all in my feels and contemplating if I made the right decision. I'm not feeling better or even stronger. I know this "relationship" is coming to an end for real this time.

I respond with: "Aww that was really sweet *tear face emoji*. Thank you! Safe travels tomorrow/today."

I go to sleep knowing nothing was the same.

A few months go by:

I don't remember who reached out to who but convo went something like:

Kendall: "I'm glad to hear you're okay. I never said I wasn't talking to you tho."

Keenan: "You broke my heart with the whole 'I don't really care about you or your feelings' and you listen to some guy that don't know me at all, tell you I don't give a d*** about you. I was really in love with you. It's not my fault the flesh got weak when I was around you. I tried multiple times to fight our sexual attraction. That didn't mean I didn't care about you."

Keenan and I didn't talk much afterward. We would occasionally check on one another via social media but that form of communication even became few and far in between. I stopped checking to see if he watched a vid as frequently as I use to. I tried to quickly move on but these things take time. Day by day. One step at a time, one foot in front of the other.

"Therefore do not worry about tomorrow, for tomorrow will worry about itself. Each day has enough trouble of its own." Matthew 6:34

Growing Pains

"These things I have spoken to you, that in Me you may have peace. In the world you will have tribulation; but be of good cheer, I have overcome the world." (John 16:33 NKJV)

Growth can be painful (like a teething baby) and scary (as we may not know what to expect) as growth is often found outside of our comfort zone.

So where did I go from there? I had to go back to the starting line and regroup.

I have matured and have forgiven those who have hurt me in various ways and I have asked for forgiveness from those I have hurt over the years as well. Essentially, I'm sharing my story because I know others have, are or will go through similar experiences. This is for all parties. You are not alone and if my experiences can derail you from that false start and steer you on to better, than this will all be worth it for me. I want to shed light on another option, an option that isn't all that clear when you're in the thick of it. Feelings and soul ties tend to prolong and complicate matters but I'm here today to tell you it is quite possible to do better and be better! Friend, we can do all things through Christ who gives us strength. Remind yourself of who you are and whose you are; you are a child of the most-high, carry yourself as such and adjust your crown.

Who Am I?

"I will praise You, for I am fearfully and wonderfully made; Marvelous are Your works, And that my soul knows very well." - Psalm 139:14 (NKJV)

While living back at home, working part-time jobs, going back to school; I was just confused. I felt like my life was in shambles and I had nothing to show for all the time I felt I wasted. I was not where I envisioned I would be. I had to seriously re-evaluate my life. I was going back to school to become a NP so I could start a career. I didn't have the desire to be a nurse practitioner but I wanted to get out of this current situation and support myself. I was embarrassed being a 24 year-old college grad back at home with no career but according to my social media I had it all together. Very few people knew I moved backed to the area yet along living with my mom. This reminds me of a quote I once read from Steven Furtick's book, *Chatterbox*, which reads, "One of the main reasons we struggle with insecurity: We're comparing our behind-the-scenes with everybody else's highlight reel."

Looking back, I truly was posting my highlight reel, taking trips, clubbing, partying, and so on. but I was never exposing my struggle. That vulnerable part of me was not displayed for the world to see. I was posting for all the wrong reasons; which ultimately convicted me to take a social media hiatus.

While taking courses to get into nursing school I had a relative become very ill unexpectedly which took a toll on me. I grew worried and anxious becoming consumed with wondering if they would pull through. I felt as if I contributed to their sudden illness as just a weekend before I was with Keenan. Was this payback. Was God punishing me? I can say now, I opened up the door for the enemy to attack but our God is a good Father. Don't ever forget that. God takes what the enemy meant for evil and turns it for good. Upon arrival to the hospital we were told by MD's that it wasn't looking too good. I prayed when compelled to. I would visit often only to see someone I love sedated with tubes and machines hooked up everywhere. This was a reality check for me to seriously get my life together. People were depending on me. Life was and is bigger than me.

I had a strong impression that I needed to let Keenan go, months prior. I tip-toed around the issue and I didn't have instant obedience. Dragging my feet on the issue was like me lining up for the 100m Dash and coming out the blocks jogging. Trying to please God and do my own thing simultaneously just caused hurt and chaos, ultimately I had to die to self. I had to allow Him to take the lead and coach me in this race of life. Purpose over pleasure. In my efforts to get it together things started happening that made it even more difficult. The enemy isn't going after those who are already living haphazardly. Those people are making a mess on their own accord so he's not focusing on them so-to-speak. In the words of David Alan Campbell: "The devil won't bother you while you're living in sin, he'll bother you when you're trying to get out."

My family member slowly recovered; it took months of going in and out of the hospital, me crying out to God for their healing, which brought me closer to Him as a servant. I helped where I could (those nursing courses and rehabilitation experience were coming in handy) and I was beginning to enjoy the progress that was being made slowly but surely.

I realized I had lost myself while trying to live up to other's expectations; expectations that did not line up with God's will. I had to recenter and refocus on my race as I had started running the race others. Compromising my beliefs and what I knew to be true. Although I was committed to celibacy, I would continue to go out and turn up for certain events. The turn ups I partook of dwindled down tremendously but I always felt wrong when I did participate. Although I was changing, I didn't want to lose my college friends; I didn't want their roles in my life to necessarily change. Especially since I felt I had finally made lifelong friends.

Needless to say, I ended up losing some friends after all. Some just grew apart with distance and time; no falling out, still cordial but with less interaction. One friendship in particular blindsided me; it was the hit I didn't see coming. This was painful to deal with as this friend was there through all my college drama. They were very familiar and in the know. They would ask about my life, or reality show rather, on a regular basis and I would spill all the tea. They enjoyed my soap opera drama and I enjoyed sharing. Hindsight tells me, however they were aiding and abetting. They enjoyed my drama, anyone's drama really. When I started to make a noticeable change, so did our friendship dynamic. It took a serious turn of events for me to realize I had put my friends on a pedestal. I had cared more about what they thought of me and how they perceived me more than what I knew God was beckoning me towards. Since I thought this friendship was going to be one of those forever friendships; imagine my surprise when it ended abruptly. In fairness, they probably didn't believe it was even that deep; but I was cut deep.

The timing of it all was abrupt to me but God works everything for the good of those who love the Lord. I was baffled and depressed, initially, feeling as if I lost a piece of myself when this falling out occurred; not realizing I was placing validation in the wrong place. It took that fallout to get to the root of the problem, to reveal this unknowing struggle to me and to eventually begin the healing process. I had to forgive while I was still hurt, upset and without receiving an "apology" from my "attacker."

I was unveiled to the truth that where I was going I didn't need to be around people who would aid and abet but those who would correct me out of love and push me towards God's purpose for my life. When I climbed out of my feelings and seriously evaluated the friendship; I realized this needed to come to an end whether I liked it or not. Little did I know I was on my way to being surrounded by women who would pour into me; but first, I had to make room. I went through a season when I was alone but not lonely. God used this season to show Himself as my constant companion, unwavering, and faithful, despite the betrayal I felt from said friend.

In reality, I was making room for more but at that time I was perceiving it as heartbreak. I didn't see how this could turn to good while in it. I lost a close friend but gained sisters in Christ. This reminds me of a YouTube video I recently watched entitled "Wavy Faith" of the Crazy Faith series by Pastor Michael Todd. He stated "Don't label something in a storm too early, give it time to develop... Maybe the scene of your greatest storm is also the setting of your greatest miracle."

I share all of this to prompt you to re-evaluate your circle. Who is holding you accountable?

"Surround yourself with people who bring out the God in you. ... Certain things are contagious." – Pastor Steven Furtick

Give Me Faith

And the apostles said to the Lord, "Increase our faith." – Luke 17:5 (NKJV)

Love Thy Self: If you can't stand being around you, how do you expect someone else to?

As I enjoy this current season of my life, I embrace the things singleness has to offer that marriage does not. For example, not having to answer to anyone but God, being able to pick up and leave as I desire, travel, hang out with family and friends when I please and as long as I please. I don't have a husband and children to consider when making personal decisions or even little things such as shopping which is a sense of freedom in itself. Take a moment and just bask in the blessing of being single.

I have more time to spend with family, friends, serve, try new things and spend with God uninterrupted and unbothered. This is a time for me to cultivate what God has placed inside of me, like this book. The struggle I experience to get this book out while single, I don't know how I would have managed this task, married with kids. I'm blessed to be able to understand the importance of this season of singleness; as I'm learning new things about myself daily and my purpose for this season. I know my husband will be in alignment with me, as I with him and we will be a force to be reckoned with, the kind of couple that make hell nervous. Until that time comes I will stay in my lane, be about my Father's business and keep working on myself.

I know I am whole without a man. In other words: I don't need a man to complete me. I do, however, have the desire to be married to a God-fearing man and to have children. In due time, God's time, that will all come to past. I want to iterate how important it is that we come into relationships whole, as two broken individuals do not complete one another but can cause more damage. Hurt people hurt people. Do whatever it is you need to do to become your best-self beforehand like counseling, better control of your finances, healthy lifestyle, etc. I believe we should seek to complement one another, not complete one another. As Neyo once said "I'm good all by myself but we're a force when we're together."

"You're not overlooked but hidden...valuable things are hidden."
- Mia Fields

Remember that when you feel overlooked, abandoned, rejected, etc. You are hidden. You are valuable. You don't leave valuable things out and about. No, you cherish them and keep them in a safe place, but in order to get to this level of contentment I had to acknowledge, release and work on myself.

I had to acknowledge there was some issues I needed to address within me. Ignoring them would not bring me healing but bringing them to God would free me if I allowed it. I had to ask God for forgiveness and for Him to reveal my heart. I noticed I played a bigger role than what I was initially willing to admit. On top of that, I was not guarding my heart properly.

Once I acknowledged there was an issue and I took responsibility for the role I played, I had to ask for forgiveness and release that hurt. I had to walk in forgiveness which required daily faith and a constant renewing of my mind. I am now able to embrace my season of singleness. I understand everyone's journey is different but I would like to share some more of my journey that you may apply as you see fit. Working on me was a gut punch at times but the work I invested in myself did not return void.

Girl, that's a Soul Tie

Growing up in the church I was familiar with the phrase "soul tie" but was never entirely sure what it was so I filled in the blanks using the context clues provided to me. I constantly heard soul ties used in a negative tone, as if it was something terrible to have. Which it can be if formed with the wrong person but all soul ties are not bad. The wrong ones can keep us from experiencing God's best for our lives, especially if we do not deal with them appropriately. If you're married to the right individual, however, then a soul tie is what God intended for us; it's when we do married things outside of marriage that gets us in trouble. There lies the problem…

Upon completing a quick search I came across a YouTube video entitled "Soul Ties: What they are and how to break them" by Actually Autumn. She broke down soul ties in a simplistic way which I thought was worth sharing. She defined soul tie using the two words that make up the phrase as below:

Soul = eternal, essential self

Tie = attach, fashion, feeling or experience shared by people

John Momplaisir, someone whom I stumbled upon via social media, describes soul ties as "an emotional bond that unites you to someone else." He also explains that soul ties are formed. He mentioned "Counterfeits come to counter your destiny." The definition of counterfeit is something that is made in exact imitation of something valuable or important with the intention to deceive or defraud. Keep in mind that soul ties that are bad form because you violated the specific boundaries of God. Let's pause for a moment and think: Are you crossing any lines? Simply put, if the relationship disrespects and dishonors your relationship with God you're dealing with a bad soul tie.

Signs you're dealing with a bad soul tie:

- Relationship does not honor God
- When you are questioning the relationship
  - Deep down you can hear God telling you to leave
  - God will answer but it's usually not what you want to hear

There are realms; the heavenly realm, which inhabits all things spiritual, and an earthly realm, all that you can perceive with your 5 senses.

Soul ties are spiritual, therefore, we can't see them in the natural realm. We think we can have sex with no strings attached but in reality there's no such thing. You may even be emotionally detached from that person but a bond is formed whether we choose to acknowledge it or not. This even plays down to a scientific level. Oxytocin, which is a hormone, is released from our brain with physical or intimate connections (i.e. sex, hugging, bonding with significant others) promotes attachment. With that said, soul ties are not formed solely through sex. The more you sleep with that person, the tighter the bond. You almost become addicted to that person, like a drug.

If not handled properly, you'll be carrying those soul ties into a new relationship.

Which brings me to my next point; how do you expect to give all of you to your future spouse if you are tied up to other people? There is a solution. I have so kindly provided some practical steps as I have laid out below on how to break a soul tie (some gathered from Autumn and John referenced prior):

1) Acknowledge you have a soul tie.
   a. Don't ignore the signs you asked God to send you.
   b. Deal with it NOW, nip it in the bud asap!
   c. Be mindful of what you're feeding your spirit. Listen to worship music, it's hard to be sad when you're praising Jesus.
   d. Journal. A good way to see how you've progressed over time.
2) Be intentional about cutting it.
   a. Pray! Ask God to free you. Allow the Holy Spirit to lead you.
   b. Unfollow/block the person if need be. Take a break from social media.
   c. Sticky notes – post positive declarations i.e. "I declare that all negative soul tie(s) are broken, Lord!" Words are powerful
      i. Prov. 18. 21 (NKJV) → Death and life are in the power of the tongue, And those who love it will eat its fruit.
      ii. Prov. 6:2 (NIV) → "You have been trapped by what you said, ensnared by the words of your mouth."
3) Deprive yourself of the person
   a. Psalm 131:2 → But I have calmed and quieted myself, I am like a weaned child with its mother; like a weaned child I am content.
   b. It's going to hurt but you're going to be okay

    c. Stop calling and texting them

    d. Do does not respond when they call or text you

    e. Stop monitoring their social media

    f. Remove things that remind you of the past – anything that attaches you to that person (teddy bear, old gifts, songs)

4) Fight your thoughts with the word of God.

    a. Speak the word of God. Isaiah 43:18-19

    b. Your word I have hidden in my heart, That I may not sin against You. (Psalm 119:11 NKJV)

5) Don't wait for your feelings to match. Do it and your feelings will catch up.

    a. Psalm 23:3 → He restores my soul… (Confess this!) It's God's will to restore your soul.

    b. Friendly reminder: Feelings are fickle and are not good gauges to base decisions off of.

My Personal Experience:

"Do you not know that your bodies are temples of the Holy Spirit, who is in you, whom you have received from God? You are not your own." – 1 Corinthians 6:19 NIV

I found myself thinking of Keenan often despite breaking it off to honor God with the temple he has generously loaned me. I had to set boundaries as my previous approach of visiting and telling myself that nothing would happen was unsuccessful to say the least. This was evident with my track record of few and far in between victories in regards to honoring my body. The definition of insanity is doing the same thing and expecting different results, at the time, I couldn't figure out why I could not break the cycle. Why did I fall so hard and develop such strong feelings for someone I didn't even talk to regularly?

I was living in the world and was acting of it too; I was conforming instead of allowing God to transform me. I was being led by my feelings. My feelings were in the commander seat of my heart but it did not add up to me logically. It did not fit; something wasn't right. I knew I deserved better yet I was accepting this lifestyle, I dare say enabling it. The Bible informs us to "Guard your heart for out of it flows the issues of life" (Proverbs 4:23). Silly me. I thought I could do as I please and not be impacted emotionally; I told myself "no strings attached" after ending it all with Lance. Little did I know, soul ties were being formed without my consent. I was game for the sex but I did not sign up for the soul knitting that was taking place. I was having sex with these guys because it physically felt good. It was pleasurable and ego stroking, but yet I was doing way more harm than good.

I unknowingly and unwillingly formed soul ties with these men I spent intimate time with throughout my past. Those soul ties needed to be broken, and as expected, some were stronger and harder to break. I had to learn to not fall into old patterns, keep my focus and believe that God truly has my best interest at heart. For the record, He truly does. He has great plans for us! He's not a man that He should lie.

Key things for me:

- I had to learn how to say, "No" unapologetically
- Be accountable for my actions and decisions
- Being mindful of the situations I was placing myself in.
- No longer compromise the word of God, i.e. no sex before marriage.
- Remembering God has better for me

"Care more about being precisely who God say you are than what other people think of you. Don't lose your destiny for anyone." - Unknown

Breaking Free From Sexual Strongholds: How to wait & what to wait on...

"God was never lost, you were." Pastor was absolutely right! I didn't find God, he found me. I attended a service in the fall after returning back home and the pastor's message resonated in my spirit. It hit so close to home and reminded me how much I had deprived my spirit. I went through so much unnecessary heartache and pain because I wanted to feed my lust and own selfish desires instead of carrying out God's will for my life. I prided myself in having a "man's" mentality but I was defiling my body and mind in the process. I got a thrill in having predetermined actions and responses that were cut-throat and self-centered. My high school best friend, who is male, would tell me how much of a "man" I acted when it came to my mentality; my college best friend always informed me how cold I was to the men I was involved with. My immature thinking had me believing I had the upper hand; my androgynous moreso masculine reasoning was my protection, my self-defense from being vulnerable and getting hurt, again. My spirit was starving for something deeper and more meaningful, a personal relationship with God. I was thankfully re-introduced to church by my mom, a church that would feed me spiritually. Just like our physical body requires food to survive, so does our spirit and it is fed through the word of God, the Holy Bible.

My stubbornness escorted me back to the starting line in order to see correction and begin rectifying the errors in my life. My life was destructive, a hot mess, and hurtful. Not only to myself but to others as well. I had to repent by asking for forgiveness and turning from my ways. This took maturity and prioritizing time to get back into the word of God. I kept trying to bury my past but in order to grow you must properly deal with it. I prayed, sought God, and sincerely asked for forgiveness for my sins. Thank God for grace! I'm living proof that God is real. My life has been transformed. After conforming to the ways of the world and doing me for years I finally started on command and the blessings he has bestowed on my life have grown tremendously. I am fortunate enough to be able to bless others; but I had to get right with Him first in order to experience the growth and be in a position to help others. Attempting to do things on your own will and strength will leave you stressed out, deprived of peace, tired, weary, without joy, did I say tired? But with Jesus comes peace, strength, a second-wind, joy, love, hope for more and abundant life.

Need help getting over the hump and on the right track? Proverbs 28:13 reads: "Whoever conceals their sins does not prosper, but the one who confesses and renounces them finds mercy." I'd like to leave you with some excerpts from Beth Moore's book, *Praying God's Word*:

"Please read this carefully: we are being sexually assaulted by the devil. The church must start mentioning the unmentionable and biblically address issues that are attacking our generation. God's Word applies to the strongholds of promiscuity, perversity, and pornography just as it does to any other. God is not shocked. He has the remedy. He is awaiting our humble, earnest cry for help."

"All sin is equal in the sense of eternal ramifications, but not all sin is equal in its earthly ramifications. Satan knows that sexual sin is unique in its attack and impact on the body of the individual believer. (1 Cor. 6:18-19)"

"WARNING: The moment the enemy sees that you are becoming serious about being delivered from strongholds and being freed to pursue holiness, he will turn up the heat of temptation. Be alert and stand against him; however, if you happen to fall at times in your journey toward freedom, do not quit."

"Long-term victory results from many short-term victories that finally collide, forming new habits."

Hear no evil, Speak no evil, See no evil & Regulate your thoughts

Above all else, guard your heart, for everything you do flows from it. – Proverbs 4:23

I had to be careful with what I listened to, watched and thought. At first, it was a tall order taking hold of these areas as I use to do as I please and listen, watch and think as I please. It it is vital to get these in check in order to protect your heart.

Hear

- What and who are you listening to? Is it edifying your spirit?
- Even music can have you feeling "some type of way." I had to cut back on my R&B and throw some more gospel in rotation as I found myself awakening something that needed to lie dormant for the time being. Certain music can cause one to become lustful and have sexual desires. This is not a coincidence my friend.

  E.g. Have you ever listen to a sad song and then grow sad all of sudden, for no recognizable reason?

Instead: listen to podcasts (Some of the one's I listen to are as follows: Jesus & Jollof, Woman Evolve, Joyce Meyer, Elevation, Transformation Church), Christian music playlists, audiobooks that enlighten your spirit.

Speak

- Watch what you say: "Death and life are in the power of the tongue, And those who love it will eat its fruit" (Prov 18:21 NKJV)
- Speak life. "Words satisfy the mind as much as fruit does the stomach; good talk is as gratifying as a good harvest." (Prov 18:20 MSG)

- Take action: Say affirmations daily. Write them on your mirrors, post sticky notes, etc. Encourage yourself. If you need help getting started I have provided a list for you to pull from at the end of this book.

See

- Avoid shows, movies that rouse something up in you that should be tamed.

  Some sexual content can create a desire that wasn't there. You can potentially open a door and expose yourself sub-consciously. Don't give the devil any ammo to use against you.

- You're not always aware of the poison that is slowly seeping in until the damage is done. In other words, you think you can afford to watch certain shows but it's better to be safe than sorry.

  E.g. Reality TV, the ones where there's nothing but drama, after viewing you may catch yourself ready to pop off for absolutely no reason at all...It's contagious sis, you don't want that energy

- Instead: let the Holy Spirit lead you on what shows to watch. Certain shows I will feel a conviction about and will know that's not the move for me. Watch a sermon on YouTube or better yet go work on the last thing God told you to do.

Think

- Contrary to popular belief you can control your thoughts.
- Shut those "bad" thoughts down immediately, don't dwell on them (albeit sad, self-pity, sorrow, weak, impure, etc). It's okay to have a moment but don't pitch a tent and stay there.
- I know, I know some thoughts just pop into your head but choose to redirect your thoughts, move onto something else.

Humans have 95% control over their thoughts according to research done on brain function and intrusive thoughts.

- "Finally, brothers and sisters, whatever is true, whatever is noble, whatever is right, whatever is pure, whatever is lovely, whatever is admirable – if anything is excellent or praiseworthy – think about such things." Philippians 4:8 NIV

In the Waiting...

Keep in mind, everyone may not remain in your life as some are for a season but there is a reason. According to a Dutch study completed in 2009, majority of friendships lasts for approximately 7 years which is around the time we enter into a new season of our lives (e.g. go off to college, new job, start a family, etc.). So don't beat yourself up on the various transitions and changes you will experience. Again, growth is found outside of your comfort zone.

I look forward to marrying a handsome God-fearing man, raising beautiful respectful earth-shaking children and cherishing every moment and memory made with family, friends, and loved ones. Until then, I will focus on strengthening my walk with God, remaining in His will, and being a light for others. I encourage you to not let your past dictate your future. Learn from your past and keep it moving. Perhaps you went through that experience to help someone else along the way. Don't set up camp and dwell there. Do not let anyone tell you it is too late for you. You can make it right if you allow God to work in you and through you. We have all sinned and fallen short of the glory of God (Romans 3:23 NIV) but that doesn't count us out. I highly suggest praying for the things that tempt you.

There's no better time than the present, make the most of it! I have learned to be mindful and accountable for what I say and thoughts I think. Contrary to popular belief, you can regulate your thoughts and speak life with the words you choose to use with the help of the Holy Spirit. I've learned to speak life into my situations and change my verbiage daily.

"Now faith is the assurance (title, deed, confirmation) of things hoped for (divinely guaranteed), and the evidence of things not seen [the conviction of their reality – faith comprehends as fact what cannot be experienced by the physical senses]." – Hebrews 11:1 AMP

So I will leave you with a quote that has stuck with me from a pastor of the church that helps me get back on the right track:

"It's not what you do for the Kingdom of God but what God told you to do that you do that matters." – Pastor Michael Thomas, Love & Faith Christian Fellowship

Worth The Wait

However, as it is written: "What no eye has seen, what no ear has heard, and what no human mind has conceived – the things God has prepared for those who love him – these are the things God has revealed to us by his Spirit. The Spirit searches all things, even the deep things of God.

I Corinthians 2:9-10 NIV

God has amazing plans for each of our lives that surpasses our understanding. As noted in Isaiah 55:8-9, His thoughts/ways are not our thoughts/ways but He exceeds them, we can't even imagine them #BlowYourMind. He promised to give us a hope and a future (Jeremiah 29:11). We are instructed to not grow weary while doing good for we will reap a harvest if we faint not (Gal. 6:9). Easier said than done, I know. But nobody said it would be easy, everything worth having you must work for. Also, let's remember to not dwell on our past. If God can forgive us, why is it so hard to forgive ourselves? I heard before, that rearview mirrors are smaller than windshields for a reason, to focus on what's in front of us. I know it can be scary, entering into the unfamiliar and into the unknown but that's the beauty of it, we get to trust Him fully. We are called to walk by faith and not by sight (2 Corinthians 5:7). But for those times you get in a funk or need a reminder here's some scriptures (the Word), quotes, affirmations and a YouTube playlist I put together that I've found helpful in my season of singleness. Being content and embracing this season will make the journey that much sweeter.

- This is where I start my comeback. I will spend no more time asking God why doors have been closed because I'll be too busy praising God for doors that are about to open.
- Every need in your life is pointing you to something deeper, a deeper relationship with God. -Pastor Steven Furtick
- Then you will be able to run with endurance the race that is set before you, without stumbling or falling. -Hebrews 12:1-2 NASB
- https://www.youtube.com/playlist?list=PL0XY-Vvi0o9tdicw8HHqpmj1MVDyk6x9A (Playlist title → False Start: A Record of Experiences)

Scriptures, Quotes & Affirmations:

- Don't be misled: Bad company corrupts good character" – 1 Corinthians 15:33
- "Sex can ruin a good relationship or prolong a bad one"
- "Let God make a man out of him, before you try to make a husband out of him" – Unknown
- "It is better to be single than to be in the wrong relationship. It will drain you, stress you, and be destructive to your mind. Rather be single working on me than to be wasting time on you." – Unknown
- Our heart is revealed by what we attract.
- Fornication and adultery have a common denominator, lack of self-control.

- "Throughout life people will make you mad, disrespect you and treat you bad. Let God deal with the things they do, cause hate in your heart will consume you too." – Will Smith
- Therefore, there is now no condemnation for those who are in Christ Jesus – Romans 8:1
- "It takes nothing to join the crowd. It takes everything to stand alone." – The Daily Positive
- "God puts dreams in your heart that are bigger than you so that you will rely on Him and His power." – Dr. Tony Evans
- "Let any one of you who is without sin be the first to throw a stone at her." John 8:7
- The pain you have been feeling cannot compare to the joy that is coming. Romans 8:18
- "If you ever find yourself in the wrong story, leave." – Mo Willems
- "There's always something not right about the one that's not right for you. If you pay attention you'll see it." – Unknown
- "Dating is not for mating, its for collecting data." – Unknown
- Set your standards before you start dating.
- "Respect yourself enough to walk away from anything that no longer serves you, grows you, or make you happy." – Unknown
- Then you will know the truth, and the truth will set you free. – John 8:32
- "Realize that if a door is closed, it's because what was behind it wasn't meant for you." - Unknown
- "The Lord goes before you and will be with you." – Deuteronomy 31:8
- "Don't feel pressured to do something against what you know is right to keep someone who isn't right for you."
- Victory necessitates vulnerability.
- "When we tackle obstacles, we find hidden reserves of courage and resilience we did not know we had. And it is only when we are faced with failure do we realize that these

resources were always there within us. We only need to find them and move on with our lives." – A. P.J. Abdul Kalam, former India president

- God is within her, she will not fall; God will help her at break of day. Psalm 46:5
- "For we live by faith, not by sight."2 Corinthians 5:7
- Faith can move mountains. Reference Matthew 17:20
- But whoever listens to me will live in safety and be at ease, without fear of harm." Proverbs 1:33
- "All a person's ways seem pure to them, but motives are weighed by the Lord." Proverbs 16:2
- "Premarital sex is a postdated check for postmarital unfaithfulness." – Jackie Kendall & Debby Jones, *Lady in Waiting*
- But the Lord stood with me and strengthened me. Reference 2 Timothy 4:17
- "Faith is not believing that God can. It is knowing that He will." – Ben Stein
- "Above all else, guard your heart, for everything you do flows from it." Proverbs 4:23
- Your best lay outside of your comfort zone.
- "Women experience so much needless pain when they run ahead of God's format." – Jackie Kendall & Debby Jones, *Lady in Waiting*
- Wise choices and obedience clears a path to destiny.
- "Kimmy said, 'God didn't supply all my wants when I was single. He changed my wants and supplied all my needs, better than I could have imagined.'" – Jackie Kendall & Debby Jones, *Lady in Waiting*
- A ring doesn't change your character, what practices are you implementing while single?
- "A godly man will not pressure a woman verbally, but will cherish her with his declarations of love and take her home

before they have to regret any violation of their purity." – Unknown

- Dear God,

  If today I lose my hope please remind me that your plans are better than my dreams.

- A great future doesn't require a great past.
- "Walk with the wise and become wise, for a companion of fools suffers harm." Proverbs 13:20
- "Do not be misled: 'Bad company corrupts good character.'" 1 Corinthians 15:33
- Always believe something wonderful is about to happen. – Unknown
- Don't resent your season of singleness. Embrace it.
- The joy of the Lord is your strength. Reference Nehemiah 8:10
- "Impression without expression can lead to depression." – Unknown
- Comparison feed discontentment.
- "Don't fear or resent the waiting periods in your life. These are the very gardens where the seeds of faith blossom." - Jackie Kendall & Debby Jones, *Lady in Waiting*
- Your godly character will garnish you the right attention.
- God didn't bring you this far to leave you. Reference Philippians 1:6
- Create in me a clean heart O God, and renew a right spirit within me. Psalm 51:10 (ESV)
- Don't dig up in doubt what you planted in faith.
- He is a rewarder of those who diligently seek Him. Reference Hebrews 11:6
- God surrounds me with His favor. Reference Psalm 5:12
- Lord, please give me the wisdom to know what must be done and the courage to do it. – Unknown
- "You teach people how to treat you by what you allow, what you stop, and what you reinforce." -Tony A. Gaskins Jr.

- "The heart is deceitful... and desperately wicked." Reference Jeremiah 17:9
- "There is no success, no happiness, and no fulfillment in life apart from a consistent, daily, growing relationship with Jesus through the Word." -M.E. Cravens
- What's for you will be, including marriage.
- Don't let anyone talk you out of your convictions, even if others believe they are unrealistic.
- In order to experience God's best for your life you must abide by God's word.
- "I will do what you have asked. I will give you a wise and discerning heart, so that there will never have been anyone like you, nor will there ever be." 1 Kings 3:12
- "The closer you get to Jesus and the more real He becomes to you, the more fullness of joy, peace, and purpose you'll have in your life." – *I'm Spiritual Not Religious*, David Cooper
- "Faith is based on eternal truth, not on emotional tangents." – *I'm Spiritual Not Religious*, David Cooper
- "And the Lord will turn our situations around if we trust Him, but that doesn't mean we won't ever face difficulties." – *I'm Spiritual Not Religious*, David Cooper
- "And you will seek Me and find Me, when you search for Me with all your heart." Jeremiah 29:13 NKJV
- "Your heavenly Father tenderly created you with the needs that only God can fully understand and fulfill." – Unknown
- For the Lord God is a sun and shield; The Lord bestows grace and favor and honor; No good thing will He withhold from those who walk uprightly. – Psalm 84:11 AMP
- Be careful not to give your heart away to things or people in idolatry.
- Learn to control yourself in your single season because a wedding band does not develops your self-control.
- "Do not merely listen to the word, and so deceive yourselves. Do what it says." James 1:22

- My soul finds rest in God alone. Reference Psalm 62:1
- "Walk with the wise and become wise, for a companion of fools suffers harm." Prov. 13:20
- God's best requires patience
- "Life is a place of service, Joy can be real only if people look upon their life as a service and have a definite objective in life outside themselves and their personal happiness." -Leo Tolstoy
- "Now the Lord is the Spirit, and where the spirit of the Lord is, there is freedom." 2 Corinthians 3:17
- "Open my eyes that I may see wonderful things in your law." Psalm 119:18
- "Jesus replied, 'You are in error because you do not know the Scriptures or the power of God.'"– Matthew 22:29
- The just shall live by faith. Reference Romans 1:17 (KJV)
- Whatever you do, do it all for the glory of God. Reference 1 Corinthians 10:31
- In Him we live and move and have our being. Reference Acts 17:28
- There's power in the word of God and power in what you say, speak the word of God.
- A kind spirit can open doors for you.
- I am always in the right place at the right time.
- A lack of self-control will lead to your suffering and bondage. Applying principles of the Bible leads to your freedom.
- I now release everything that is not divinely designed for me and create space for all that I deserve. – *WERK 101*, Koereyelle
- Nothing is too good to be true; nothing is too good to last when you look to God for your good. – *WERK 101*, Koereyelle
- "Doubt your doubts before you doubt your faith." - Dieter F. Uchtdort

- Stay away from negative people. They have a problem for every solution. – Unknown
- Those who move forward with a happy spirit will find that things will always work out. -Gordon B. Hunckley
- A lack of boundaries invites a lack of respect.
- The more you know who you are, and what you want, the less you let things upset you. -Stephanie Perkins
- Just cause they go to church doesn't mean they're a potential husband/wife.
- Nothing is impossible, the word itself says 'I'm Possible'!" – Audrey Hepburn
- "For God has not given us a spirit of fear and timidity, but of power, love, and self-discipline." 2 Timothy 1:7 (NLT)
- Life rooted in God stands firm. Reference Proverbs 12:3
- "God can't fill you when you are already full of yourself." - Max Lucada
- "To walk out of God's will is to step into nowhere." – C.S. Lewis
- Pray more, worry less. – Unknown
- God is calling you, equipping you, preparing you according to His purpose. Reference Psalm 138:8
- To pray is to let go and let God take over. – Unknown
- "Devote yourselves to prayer, being watchful and thankful." Colossians 4:2
- "Blessed is the man who remains steadfast under trial, for when he has stood the test he will receive the crown of Life, which God has promised to those who love Him." James 1:12 (ESV)

- I AM...

A daughter of the king. Galatians 3:26

God-fearing Proverbs 31:30

Steadfast in the love of Christ Romans 8:31-38

Redeemed Ephesians 1:7

Loved.John 3:16

Beautiful. Psalm 139:13-16

Worthy. Matthew 6:26

More than make-up and clothes. 1 Peter 3:3-4

Free. John 8:36

Worth it. Romans 5:6-8

Victorious. Philippians 4:13

Joyful. John 15:11

Transformed. Romans 12:2

Dignified. Proverbs 22:11

Favoured. Proverbs 8:35

- "Because limits, like fears, are often just an illusion." – Michael Jordan
- "I wait for the Lord, my whole being waits, and in his word I put my hope." Psalm 130:5
- "Cast your cares on the Lord and he will sustain you; he will never let the righteous be shaken." Psalm 55:22
- Trust in the Lord with all your heart; do not depend on your own understanding. Seek His will in all you do, and He will show you which path to take. Don't be impressed with your own wisdom. Instead, fear the Lord and turn away from evil. Proverbs 3:5-7
- When you take time with God and listen to His voice, he renews your strength and enables you to handle life. – Unknown
- Set your minds on things above, not on earthly things." Colossians 3:2
- "If one is not whole before marriage I must warn that marriage will not complete a broken soul." – T.D. Jakes (Promises from God for Single Women)
- "Don't entertain those things that can't satisfy our spirit and only gratify our flesh." – Tovares Grey
- Unless you win the battle in your mind first, you're setting yourself up for defeat.
- Hold onto Jesus tighter than anyone else. (Exodus 34:14)
- "If you believe, you will receive whatever you ask for in prayer." Matthew 21:22 NIV
- "When I can't see his hand I must trust His heart." – Unknown
- "You can see how much you love God by how much you listen to and obey him. – Anonymous
- Never give up on God, even if it feels like He has given up on you; you only feel that way because you only know the present and the past. It is in the future that your answered prayer lies! – Proverbs 31 Project, Melissa Calloway

- "Blessed is she who has believed that the Lord would fulfill His promises to her!" Luke 1:45
- If ye shall ask anything in my name, I will do it. John 14:14 KJV
- Create in me a pure heart, O God, and renew a steadfast spirit within me. Psalm 51:10
- But in that coming day no weapon turned against you will succeed. You will silence every voice raised up to accuse you. These benefits are enjoyed by the servants of the Lord; their vindication will come from Me. I, the Lord, have spoken! Isaiah 54:17 (NLT)
- Let everything that has breath praise the Lord. Praise the Lord. Psalm 150:6
- For where two or three are gathered together in My name, there I am in the midst of them. Matthew 18:20 (NKJV)
- Jesus said unto him, Thou shalt love the Lord thy God with all thy heart, and with all thy soul, and with all thy mind. Matthew 22:37 (KJV)
- The eyes of your understanding being enlightened; that ye may know what is the hope of his calling, and what the riches of the glory of his inheritance in the saints, And what is the exceeding greatness of His power to us-ward who believe, according to the working of His mighty power, which He wrought in Christ, when He raised Him from the dead, and set Him at His own right hand in the Heavenly places, far above all principality, and power, and might, and dominion, and ever name that is named, not only in this world, but also in that which to come: Ephesians 1:18-21 (KJV)
- And this the confidence that we have in Him, that, if we ask anything to His will, he heareth us: And if we know that He hear us, whatsoever we ask, we know that we have the petitions that we desired of Him.1 John 5:14-15 (KJV)
- What shall we then say to these things? If God be for us, who can be against us? Romans 8:31 (KJV)

- Repay no one evil for evil, but give thought to do what is honorable in the sight of all. Romans 12:17 (ESV)
- Set your mind on things above, not on earthly things. Colossians 3:2
- Wait patiently for the Lord. Be brave and courageous. Yes, wait patiently for the Lord. Psalm 27:14
- Blessed are those who keep his statutes and seek him with all their heart. Psalm 119:2
- Ye are of God, little children, and have overcome them: because greater is He that is in you, than He that is in the world. 1 John 4:4 (KJV)
- Jesus looked at them and said, "With man this is impossible, but with God all things are possible." Matthew 19:26
- Be ye not unequally yoked together with unbelievers for what fellowship hath righteousness with unrighteousness? And what communion hath light with darkness? 2 Cor. 6:14 (KJV)
- For as the body without the spirit is dead, so faith without works is dead also. James 2:26 KJV

ROMANS 8:31-37

What, then, shall we say in response to these things? If God is for us, who can be against us? He who did not spare His own son, but gave him up for us all – how will He not also, along with Him, graciously give us all things? Who will bring any charge against those whom God has chosen? It is God who justifies. Who then is the one who condemns? No one. Christ Jesus who died – more than that, who raised to life – is at the right hand of God and is also interceding for us. Who shall separate us from the Love of Christ? Shall trouble or hardship or persecution or famine or nakedness or danger or sword? As it is written: 'For your sake we face death all day long; we are considered as sheep to be slaughtered.' No, in all these things we are more than conquerors through Him who loved us."

The Ultimate Relationship

I could not end this book without giving someone the opportunity to experience a personal relationship with Jesus Christ. He died for my sins as well as yours. With that said, get in on this for tomorrow is not promised. The Holy Bible says no one can come to the Father except through Him. He is the way, the truth and the life (John 14:6). If you're looking to start the absolute best journey of your life you can start by confessing and believing that God raised Jesus from the dead (Romans 10:9). If you're coming back to God, that's perfectly fine too! You may relate to the Prodigal Son (Luke 15:11-32). So let's say this prayer out loud:

Heavenly Father, I ask that you come into my life and make me brand new. I repent of all my sins and I thank you for sending your son, Jesus who knew no sin, to die for my sins. I believe in my heart that you have raised Jesus from the dead and sent the Holy Spirit to dwell in me. Thank you for saving me.

After saying the prayer I highly recommend getting connected to a word-based church. Tell someone you've just been born again/rededicated your life back to God. While on earth Jesus said, "if you'll be ashamed to own me I'll be ashamed to own you" (Luke 9:26).

I'm so proud of you and I will be praying for you! God loves us with an everlasting love and truly has our best interest at heart. Your best days are ahead. Remember to trust the process and run your race. Welcome to new beginnings!

"Therefore, if anyone is in Christ, the new creation has come. The old has gone, the new is here!" 2 Corinthians 5:17

Love,

Tay Monét

Let's Connect

TayMonet.com

Social Media Platforms: @TayMonet_com